POWER
POLITICS

POWER POLITICS

Trump and the Assault on American Democracy

DARRELL M. WEST

BROOKINGS INSTITUTION PRESS

Washington, D.C.

Copyright © 2022
THE BROOKINGS INSTITUTION
1775 Massachusetts Avenue, N.W.
Washington, D.C. 20036
www.brookings.edu

The Brookings Institution is a private nonprofit organization devoted to research, education, and publication on important issues of domestic and foreign policy. Its principal purpose is to bring the highest quality independent research and analysis to bear on current and emerging policy problems. Interpretations or conclusions in Brookings publications should be understood to be solely those of the authors.

Library of Congress Control Number: 2022933044

ISBN 9780815739593 (hardcover)
ISBN 9780815739609 (ebook)

9 8 7 6 5 4 3 2 1

Typeset in Bookmania and Oswald

Composition by Elliott Beard

To all the reporters, professors, experts, advocates, and ordinary citizens
who are working to protect American democracy.

Contents

1

Introduction

We live during a tumultuous time. Both in the United States and around the world, large-scale transformations are endangering democratic processes and threatening basic liberties. Authoritarianism is taking root in many nations as people turn to strong leaders who vow to end chaos, chart a firm path, and restore stability.

This is not the first time humanity has faced major governance problems. During World War II, the old order was destroyed and a number of economies were devastated. Yet leaders came together afterward, constructed new regimes, and negotiated treaties and agreements, and life grew more calm and peaceful.

At many points in history, unsettling developments have spiraled out of control and plunged individual nations and the world as a whole into devastating turmoil. During those periods, there was ineffective governance, leaders turned dictatorial, and problems got much worse.

In this book, I argue that we sit at a crucial crossroads where governance could move in a variety of different directions. We can seize the moment, demand constructive changes, and shift toward a brighter future, or we can fail to deal with rising threats and have our current system crumble. It is hard to see America being able to solve domestic problems or lead the world internationally if we do not function in an effective manner. Having deficiencies in terms of electoral processes, voting rights, public opinion, political institutions, media coverage, civic discourse, and social media dissemination is the epitome of ineffective and dysfunctional governance. It is time to recognize the seriousness of these problems and take actions to protect cherished rights and processes.

Threats to American Democracy

The United States faces extraordinary problems of polarization, extremism, and radicalization, which make it difficult to safeguard our democratic system and deal with important policy issues. In recent decades, there has been a precipitous decline of public confidence in government, along with problems of institutional performance and questions regarding election integrity. Taken together, these developments pose systemic risks and threaten the very fabric of our democracy, society, and politics.[1]

Many of these issues were highlighted during and after the 2020 election. Boasting the highest voter turnout in nearly one hundred years, the contest revealed sharp divisions, frayed civility, a widespread mistrust of political opponents, and efforts at raw political power. The results in both the presidential and the congressional elections showed a polarization and radicalization that permeated many parts of the country and will likely reverberate for the foreseeable future.

The country was fortunate during this critical time that courageous public officials from each party stepped up to defend democracy and safeguard electoral procedures. State and local elections administrators overcame intense political pressure to count the votes, audit the results, and certify popular vote winners. In particular, there were a number of Democratic and Republican governors, secretaries of state, and local elections officials as well as judges in key swing states who resisted partisan overtures and upheld election laws. But without their principled actions, America could have experienced a far more tumultuous presidential transition.

There are many developments that have intensified America's contemporary political turmoil.[2] As an example, the near extinction of moderates in Congress has had detrimental consequences for governance and problem solving. Bargaining, compromise, and negotiation used to be the guiding principles for American politicians. Legislators sought to resolve conflict and forge winning coalitions that cut across a variety of perspectives.

Yet, as I note later in this volume, institutional dysfunction, changes in public opinion, the rise of toxic social media platforms, the power of big money, and the incentives that political leaders have to keep their supporters angry have poisoned the atmosphere for reasoned discussions and effective governance. Politicians fight with everything they have, and policymaking has become more a matter of might than right. The information ecosystem rewards those who are angry by amplifying their messages and spreading narratives of hate and vitriol. As noted by Indiana University political scientist Steven Webster, "Politicians seek to make their supporters angry because angry voters are loyal voters."[3]

In the current climate, there is a clear formula by which leaders can subvert elections and democracy. They can allege ballot fraud, demand an audit, throw out contested ballots from certain areas, get the state legislature to certify the victory, and have Congress ratify that decision.[4] And once in power, such leaders can use democratic processes to pass legislation that rigs future elections, packs the judiciary, gerrymanders legislative districts, undermines public trust in the media, and delegitimizes the professors, think tank scholars, and nonprofit experts who document those actions.

The United States has already moved several steps down the path of illiberalism, and it won't take much to slide into outright authoritarianism. We live in a risky time where transformational shifts can take place quickly. It is important to prepare for a variety of scenarios as the country navigates the shifting sands of political, social, economic, demographic, and institutional changes. Despite our two-century tradition of self-rule, the reassuring admonition that "it can't happen here" is no longer very convincing.

Alternative Explanations

There are many viewpoints about what has gone wrong with American democracy. In a widely read essay, Brookings scholar Robert Kagan places much of the blame on Donald Trump. He says the leader created a cult of personality around himself, and there is a coming constitutional crisis generated by the former president's willingness to push lies regarding election integrity, violate long-held democratic norms, and play to the fears and resentments of the American heartland. Each of those actions poses considerable risks in upcoming elections and puts the country in a precarious position.[5]

In this extraordinary situation, though, risks emanating from Trump, although quite substantial, may not represent the full story. There are many problems that confront American democracy from counter-majoritarian political institutions, the existence of fake news and alternative realities, and culture wars that enrage people and make it difficult to solve problems. In some respects, Trump is a symptom of underlying problems in American politics and society, not the ultimate cause.

In this vein, some observers point to longer-term developments that predate and go beyond Trump. For example, a number cite a Republican party that has been taken over by ultranationalist forces and appears willing to do whatever it takes to gain power. In a 2012 book, *It's Even Worse Than It Looks: How the American Constitutional System Collided with the New Politics of Extremism*, scholars Thomas Mann and Norman Ornstein warn about a GOP engaging in "asymmetric polarization" and moving toward becoming an insurgent party with antidemocratic views. Writing several years before Trump's presidency, they perceptively argued that Republican leaders have previously engaged in actions that threaten American democracy.[6]

Yet conservatives say liberals have contributed to political polarization and extremism by moving Democrats to the left.[7] They argue progressive voices have grown emboldened to call for major change in social policy and political processes. A number of progressive leaders feel the country has been on the wrong path for decades, and now is the time to chart a different course. As that bloc has grown in power and intensity, many Democrats have pushed bigger and bolder solutions and, in conjunction with conservatives shifting to the right, the gap between the two parties has grown dangerously wide.

Still others focus on long-term structural forces that have created social and economic tensions that are very difficult for any political leaders to resolve.[8] Income inequality is at a one-hundred-year high, economic opportunity has diminished for many Americans, geographic disparities are widespread between the U.S. heartland and the coasts, racial and gender injustices persist, technology innovation is disrupting whole sectors of the economy, and geopolitical tensions are high around the world. The sheer magnitude of these challenges has pushed democratic governance to the breaking point and made it impossible for anyone to resolve conflict and govern effectively.

Finally, some writers emphasize systemic factors that enable political illiberalism to flourish. In her insightful book, *Twilight of Democracy: The Seductive Lure of Authoritarianism*, Anne Applebaum notes how illiberal leaders "use conspiracy theory, political polarization, social media, and even nostalgia" to overturn democracy and institute illiberal or authoritarian regimes. Such individuals question facts, harass opponents, undermine civil society, and weaken oversight institutions so there is little accountability for themselves.[9] Taken together, these shifts make it easy for illiberal leaders to take advantage of chaos and disorder by promising a strong hand that will steady the ship.

It matters which of these perspectives is most important because the remedies vary substantially across these possible explanations. If Trump is the problem, for example, the solution is not to elect him as president again. However, if the malady lies with polarization and extremism fueled by Republicans moving to the right and Democrats shifting to the left, the redress is not just stopping Trump but figuring out how to deal with radicalized political parties.

Yet, if the problems are more structural and systemic in nature, as I argue in this book, the correctives must be far broader. It is not simply a matter of stopping Trump and copycat candidates, or having more moderates in each party, but rather addressing the institutional, societal, economic, and technological forces that are endangering governance and democracy. Those kinds of cures involve broad-based political reform, dealing with income inequality, addressing racism, and coping with the ills of widespread technological change.

The challenge right now is a perfect storm where all these factors are coming together in dangerous ways. Each development feeds on other maladies and exacerbates societal tensions, institutional dysfunction, and political norm busting. For example, social media and income inequality endanger democracy, yet poor governance makes it impossible to mitigate problems created by these platforms and the loss of economic opportunity. American democracy is at risk because of not just one but many factors that are straining the ability of politicians to address major problems. Some threats emanate from Trump and nationalist elements within the Republican party, whereas others arise from Democrats shifting to the left, structural economic inequality, and cultural tensions. Problems in each area fuel a sense of grievance on the part of many people, generate feelings that "the other side" is not playing fairly, and encourage leaders to use raw political power to accomplish their political objectives.[10] Left unchecked, it will not take much of a political crisis to delegitimize elections, overwhelm governing processes, and topple democracy.

Why Trumpism Will Outlast Trump

It is easy to blame Donald Trump for the threats to democracy. After all, he abused the powers of his executive office, spread false claims, incited violence, and tried to rig the election in his favor. He violated major ethics norms, claimed he was above the law, and argued he could not be indicted for any crimes while serving as chief executive.

But it is important to realize that Trumpism will likely outlast Trump himself.[11] The structural forces he appealed to existed in society well before he became president and almost certainly will endure after he is gone from the political scene. He may have accelerated societal discontent and a sense of grievance on the part of some Americans, but he did not create that resentment. Discontent has been present for a long time and shaped the polarization and extremism that have built up over several decades.[12]

The discontent is manifest in many issues, ranging from abortion and immigration to the loss of economic opportunity, critical race theory, and what it means to be an American. Recent populist uprisings, such as the tea party, antiglobalization sentiments, anti–Wall Street viewpoints, climate change skepticism, antivaccination and antimasking behaviors, and Trumpism itself signal the existence of widespread dissatisfaction that may take years to resolve. Given the magnitude of the forces at play, it will be difficult to ease our public fissures, reduce polarization, diminish extremism, and improve our information ecosystem.

With these current problems, many do not trust experts and feel that coastal elites have sold the heartland down the river. They point to unfair policies, flawed trade deals, and widespread geographic disparities to buttress their feeling that the system is rigged and ordinary folks are disadvantaged. With people being deeply cynical about contemporary affairs and distrusting political opponents, it will take considerable effort for the country to work through the intense and highly partisan conflict that emanates from long-term, structural forces.

My Unique Vantage Point

I have a unique vantage point from which to assess the contemporary crisis of American democracy. For much of my adult life, I taught political science at Brown University. Coming to that institution near the beginning of Ronald Reagan's presidency, I witnessed the growing polarization in American politics and brought an analytic lens to how toxicity was poisoning civic discourse and altering both public opinion and electoral behavior.

I had grown up on a dairy farm in rural Ohio and understood the frustrations of those living in the heartland. Most of my relatives and many of my high school friends were conservatives who did not like what had transpired over the past several decades. They saw the two coasts thriving while the heartland struggled. They felt the system was rigged against them, and media and cultural elites looked down on them. And as religious people, they disliked what they saw as the growing secularization of the United States and the loss of traditional moral values.[13]

At many points in time, my life seemed schizophrenic as I navigated the vast gulf between my conservative roots and teaching at one of the most liberal universities in America. Brown was so liberal I sometimes joked that the political divide on campus was not between Democrats and Republicans (which were a rare breed at Brown), but between Democrats and Socialists. It was not that the latter were so numerous but that they were a noisy presence on campus and had an outsized influence on campus dialogues.[14]

In 2008, my life turned in still another unexpected direction when I moved to Washington, D.C., to head the Governance Studies program at the Brookings Institution. It was a think tank that was the epitome of the eastern establishment. Each week, we hosted leading politicians, reporters, business leaders, and academic experts for discussions about American politics and domestic policy. Joining a think tank in the capitol city gave me a bird's-eye perspective on the massive upheavals that were unfolding and the risks that were growing at an alarming pace.

Throughout this volume, I combine my perspective as a political scientist studying long-term trends in American politics with my personal experiences growing up in the Bible Belt, teaching at a liberal university, and working in a D.C. think tank. I draw on my own encounters as well as those of my acquaintances, the experiences of people at other think tanks and universities, and what has happened to those who operate in advocacy organizations and nonprofit groups. Having taught at a leading university for many years and worked at a think tank for more than a decade, I have an uncommon position from which to analyze current threats and dangers.

Overview of the Book

The plan of the book is as follows. Chapter 2 discusses developments that have created a poisonous atmosphere in American democracy. The storming of the U.S. Capitol on January 6, 2021, shocked many observers and led to fears regarding the future of the political system. But the country's problems are far more acute than what occurred on that date. I discuss the many ways in which contemporary features, such as shifts in voting rights, presidential emergency power declarations, the Insurrection Act of 1807, and the Electoral Count Act of 1887, can provide a future means by which "legal coups" could happen in the United States. January 6, 2021, could be a harbinger of far more worrisome political risks.

Chapter 3 examines the changing American political and media landscape. Information is being weaponized and used to disrupt governance. Changes in digital technology have created enormous cyber vulnerabilities across all parts of the ideological spectrum and made it easy for those of various political stripes to engage in personal destruction of their opponents. Lies and propaganda are easily spread via social media, and at a time of widespread polarization, it is hard to have reason-based discussions about major policy problems. All these developments undermine qualities of civil society that are vital for democratic governance.

Chapter 4 reviews the many currents in public opinion that are threatening democracy. There is a high level of political polarization, widespread mistrust in government, declining support for democracy among the general public, and a worrying emergence of authoritarian viewpoints among a significant part of the electorate. Those developments create a public opinion climate that could enable extraconstitutional actions on the part of ambitious leaders.

Chapter 5 outlines how the emergence of counter-majoritarian political processes and institutions have made it possible for small groups of people to gain power over broader interests. There are ways in which the Electoral College, U.S. Senate, legislative gerrymandering, federal court packing, and campaign finance abuses have led to an unrepresentative system and the undermining of democracy itself. Raw power exercised by small numbers of people makes the general public quite cynical about public affairs and affects the ability of the overall system to address important problems.

Chapter 6 outlines forces in the knowledge sector that have increased the complexity and intensity of political conflict. There are issues related to the role of money, the rise of partisanship, hardball tactics, fake news, and changes in geopolitics. At a time of tidal-wave shifts in domestic politics and international affairs, it is easy for conflict to intensify and for universities, think tanks, and non-profit organizations to come under fire. It is quite challenging for university professors and think tank experts to navigate the vicissitudes of contemporary politics.

Chapter 7 discusses how the use of private investigators and government inquiries creates problems for individual reputations, civil society organizations, and democratic discourse. In a digital world, it is easy to gain access to confidential information that can embarrass opponents, weaken them politically, or expose them to legal harm. In combination with instantaneous dissemination by social media and partisan news sites, it is a treacherous environment for those who participate in or analyze the process.

Chapter 8 discusses the risks of societal shaming during a period when social media can spread information, misinformation, and disinformation around the world in seconds. Online vitriol and personal attacks can endanger livelihoods and even lives and can also undermine public discussions. Digital technologies have sped up the news cycle, threatened public health, raised the systemic risks, and undermined the fabric of civic dialogue.

Chapter 9 covers the culture wars that have angered voters on all sides and made it difficult to address pressing problems. Leaders pit groups against one another in dangerous ways, wedge issues are used for political purposes, and societal tensions are exploited in harmful ways. Those developments enrage people and increase societal discord. Widespread unhappiness makes it difficult to take actions that might reduce social inequities, decrease conflict, and mitigate policy problems.

Chapter 10 offers advice for dealing with this high-risk situation where democracy is under assault and authoritative institutions are under suspicion. I outline how we need to protect people, organizations, and the country as a whole from the challenges that permeate the existing environment. It is important to understand the risks of poor governance, address the dangers of digital communications, and see how legal, media, policy, and political changes are undermining personal and systemic protections. I outline a number of steps we need to take in order to secure democracy, reason-based discourse, fair play, and procedural justice during a threatening time.

2

Why You Should Be Worried

People's fears about democracy have risen in recent years due to several developments. There have been violent outbursts that have shocked people and shattered long-standing norms. In addition, the opaqueness of legal procedures and institutional processes surrounding both elections and governance poses risks for civil society and the political system. There are worrisome trends in civic discourse that debase our discussions and make it difficult to take constructive actions. Given these developments, it is crucial to understand why people should be worried about our political system and the ways perfectly legal coups can take place in the United States.

Open Insurrection

On January 6, 2021, the day when members of Congress met officially to certify the 2020 vote and name Joe Biden as the chief executive, the then president Donald Trump was upset at what he saw as an epic unfairness committed against him and his supporters. All those who opposed him and his plan to make America great again had rigged the presidential election by engaging in massive ballot fraud. Even though more than sixty judges, including a number appointed by Trump himself, had rejected these accusations on grounds of insufficient evidence, the chief executive continued to spread the lie that opponents had stolen the election. He was angry at the blatant miscarriage of justice and wanted to give a public talk to his followers on the National Mall right outside the White House.

However, his address that day would turn out to be no typical presidential speech. Trump would rant as he always did and say it was time to "stop the steal." He played his usual grievance card that he was the object of tremendous unfairness and told his devotees they were patriotic people who had supported his efforts to reform America. He could not believe how treacherous Democrats were and the lengths to which they would go to undermine him and engage in unfair tactics. His aides and numerous other people had heard those complaints many times since Election Day.[1]

In an improvised section at the end of his speech, he implored the crowd to move down to the U.S. Capitol. In language that shocked many people, he uttered the now famous admonition: "After this, we're going to walk down—and I'll be there with you. We're going to walk down. We're going to walk down. Any one you want, but I think right here. We're going to walk down to the Capitol, and we're going to cheer on our brave senators and congressmen and women. We're probably not going to be cheering so much for some of them because you'll never take back our country with weakness. You have to show strength, and you have to be strong."[2]

As Trump departed the stage, his agitated chief of staff, Mark Meadows, confronted him and the security detail: "There's no way we are going to the Capitol." The president feigned a lack of understanding about why his top aide was upset. He pretended that he didn't grasp what Meadows was proclaiming. His adviser repeated the president's words: "You said you were going to march with them to the Capitol." "Well—," Trump replied, and then paused, seemingly uncertain how to respond. "How would we do that? We can't organize that. We can't," the chief of staff implored him. "I didn't mean it literally" was Trump's disingenuous response. Technically, the executive was correct that he did not intend to tag along with the marchers on their route to the Capitol. Yet the president knew exactly what he was doing when he urged his followers to confront lawmakers. Despite having lost the popular vote and Electoral College, he was deadly serious about remaining in power and thought a massive public protest would help his cause.[3]

Meadows was worried that his tempestuous boss had added those exhortations to the crowd. The chief of staff understood that within hours members of Congress were going to certify Biden's victory, thereby ensuring Trump's defeat, and he did not want his boss anywhere near that location. He knew that Trump and his sometimes lawyer Rudy Giuliani had spent weeks hatching one scheme after another in an effort to keep Trump in office. Meadows was familiar with the planning because he was involved with a number of the options, such as the efforts to overturn the results of key states by alleging ballot fraud.[4]

Trump did not head to the Capitol as promised, but instead went back to the White House. There was a lunch with family members and close aides. Afterward, Trump watched the unfolding march on television, although he was unhappy that only the public affairs network C-SPAN was covering it live. None of the major broadcast networks or cable stations were showing the angry crowd streaming down Pennsylvania Avenue.

Early in the afternoon, Trump tweeted out his dismay that his own vice president, Mike Pence, had failed to object to Democrat Joe Biden's election victory, effectively making him president. "Mike Pence didn't have the courage to do what should have been done to protect our Country and our Constitution, giving States a chance to certify a corrected set of facts, not the fraudulent or inaccurate ones which they were asked to previously certify. USA demands the truth!" Trump wrote.[5] He could not believe his own running mate had refused to back his claims about massive ballot fraud and a stolen election. Up until the end, he thought there was a chance the vice president would upend centuries of democratic precedent and disapprove Biden's victory.

Trump's followers did exactly what he had urged them to do. They marched to the legislative citadel and were mad as hell. They agreed with the New York billionaire that the election had been rigged by Democrats and Trump had been robbed of a rightful victory. Egged on by conservative television networks, partisan websites, and inflammatory social media posts, they sided with Trump's view that a dramatic theft had occurred, and they were going to express their profound discontent with that injustice.[6]

The crowd was filled with protesters who believed what Trump said. They wore MAGA hats, carried American flags, and were upset at the injustice. They were "the base," the part of America that loved Trump and stayed with him regardless of what critics said. Indeed, the more extreme his behavior, the more his people loved him.

Mixed in with the assemblage, though, were operatives who had prepared for this very moment and saw it as an extraordinary opportunity to fight back against all the abuses being committed against conservatives by progressives, minorities, professional women, immigrants, news reporters, and policy advocates. There were members of the Oath Keepers as well as the Proud Boys, ultranationalist organizations dedicated to putting America back on the desired course, even if they had to do so through violence. Representatives from militia groups across the nation had trained with assault weapons and riled one another up with talk about a pending civil war between progressive and ultranationalist forces.[7]

When those paramilitary forces reached the Capitol, they did not engage in peaceful protest on behalf of their favored candidate, as many Americans had done over the years. That was a guaranteed right to freedom of expression that had been a cherished part of the

Constitution's Bill of Rights. Many patriotic citizens had protested on behalf of a favored cause or individual.

Rather than peacefully expressing their discontent, hundreds in the angry mob breached the Capitol barriers, shattered windows, broke down doors, and quickly overpowered the outmanned Capitol Police force. They entered the building looking for blood. "Where's Nancy?" they shouted, referring to Democratic House Speaker Nancy Pelosi, with the implied threat of violence against her. Others were more explicit in their intentions when they shouted, "Hang Mike Pence," because he had not sided with Trump on this crucial day. Indeed, someone had constructed a platform with a hangman's noose on the Mall outside the legislative hall.[8]

For hours, the mob rampaged throughout the Capitol building. They forced members of the House and Senate to suspend their certification procedure and seek refuge under police protection. They invaded Nancy Pelosi's office and put their feet up on her desk, while also looting personal items from key spaces. They posed for pictures on the House dais, where the Speaker presided over official proceedings. They riffled through senators' personal papers, which in the haste to exit the chamber, had been left on top of most members' desks.

This was an open insurrection against the national government, one of the ugliest and most violent of the last century. It would upend long-cherished norms and values of U.S. democracy and violate key tenets regarding the peaceful transfer of power. Not only did it signal that American democracy was under serious attack, it would test the country's ability to withstand dark forces that had been building over a number of years.

The whole scene upset one top military leader who worked under Trump. General Mark Milley, the Joint Chiefs of Staff chairman, was gravely concerned by what he was witnessing. For some time, Milley had seen Trump as a "classic authoritarian leader with nothing to lose. He described to aides that he kept having this stomach-churning feeling that some of the worrisome early stages of twentieth-century fascism in Germany were replaying in twenty-first-century America. He saw parallels between Trump's rhetoric about election fraud and Adolf Hitler's insistence to his followers at the Nuremberg rallies that he was both a victim and their savior." Shocked by what he saw that January day, Milley ominously warned his aides, "This is a Reichstag moment. . . . The gospel of the Führer."[9]

Legislators would survive the violent assault, but in an equally disturbing development, there were 139 House GOP members and 8 Republican senators that evening who supported at least one objection to Biden's Electoral College certification. They claimed that they just wanted to have a debate on ballot fraud, but the truth appeared far more threatening. Despite having no serious evidence of voting irregularities that would have altered the election outcome in any state, they used the vote certification process (which in the past had been primarily a ceremonial occasion) to openly challenge the legitimacy of Biden's victory.[10]

Months later, when Democrats sought a bipartisan commission to investigate the events of January 6th, as had happened after the September 11, 2001, terrorist attacks, most Republican legislators refused to vote for it. They did not want detailed hearings, legal subpoenas, and public testimony regarding what had happened and how the nation had reached that sad point. They preferred to bury those topics and move national discussions on to more advantageous political grounds. It was safer, they reasoned, to let the insurrection pass without detailed analysis than to delve deeply into its planning, operations, financing, and execution.[11]

The GOP's stunning response to the entire ordeal represents a vivid indication of the way future elections could spiral out of control under the guise of allegations regarding voting misdeeds.[12] While the Biden process followed the letter of the law and Congress ultimately certified his victory, there were precedents set in the ascertainment proceedings that in the years ahead could allow either states or members of Congress to certify Electoral College votes that run counter to the popular results in those places. That is exactly why Trump's allegations of ballot fraud constituted such a risky threat; it is one of the vehicles through which later candidates could unfairly gain or retain the top office in the land.

For me personally, that January day represented a shocking turn of events as I watched the violent activities on television from my home not far from the Federal Triangle. I had moved to D.C. in 2008 as Barack Obama was coming to power. It was an eventful time as Democrats tried to remake policy following the George W. Bush presidency. There were efforts under the new leader to provide greater access to health care, improve educational opportunity, and raise taxes on the wealthy. With the country's first African American president, commentators openly spoke about a time of hope and bipartisanship, and America moving into a postracial society based on inclusivity and justice for all.

Those predictions proved to be wildly inaccurate. Not only did major political and racial divisions persist, the Obama presidency generated a dramatic backlash in 2016. To the surprise of virtually everyone, Donald Trump won the Electoral College while losing the popular vote. As president, he reversed a great deal that Obama had accomplished. He pushed policies that gave tax cuts to the rich, built a wall along the southern border with Mexico, rolled back environmental regulations, pulled the country out of the Paris climate accords, weakened the transatlantic relationship with Europe, came within one vote in the Senate of repealing Obamacare, and threatened the entire democratic enterprise.

Legal Coups

The shifting American landscape deserves attention because there is nothing guaranteed about the survival of democratic regimes. In their prescient 2019 volume, *How Democracies Die*, Harvard professors Steven Levitsky and Daniel Ziblatt discuss the "steady weakening of critical institutions, such as the judiciary and the press, and the gradual erosion of long-standing political norms."[13] Relying on evidence from European and Latin American democracies that were replaced by authoritarianism, they note how quickly this can happen and why no one should be complacent regarding our current state of affairs.

In the contemporary environment, legal coups are possible in the United States in at least four specific ways: (1) the Insurrection Act of 1807 (which gives presidents the unilateral ability to put state or federal military troops on the street in order to quell disorder), (2) emergency power declarations that provide executives with virtually unlimited powers to act in a national emergency and to do so unilaterally without much recourse by Congress or the courts, (3) voting restrictions that disproportionately advantage one of the political parties, and (4) the Electoral Count Act of 1887 (which governs how Congress certifies Electoral College votes and resolves disputed presidential elections and allegations of vote fraud).

Of course, these are not the only options for undemocratic actions. It is possible for malevolent leaders to politicize the Justice Department, hijack the military for illicit political purposes, use law enforcement to harass and jail opponents, weaken the ability of journalists to hold leaders accountable, subvert the impartiality of the judiciary, and delegitimize civil society organizations so it is hard for them to hold leaders accountable.[14]

But these four vehicles are currently on the books, are so open-ended they could be subject to profound abuse, and face few limits on their utilization. Those qualities make them especially dangerous during a polarized time. In the hands of unscrupulous leaders, they can be misused in ways that endanger the entire political system.

For example, the Insurrection Act was passed by Congress early in the nation's history as a way to empower the chief executive to deal with popular uprisings. At that point, there had already been discontent in the form of revolutionary troops who were upset over not getting paid; Shay's Rebellion in 1786, which arose over aggressive tax collection in Massachusetts; the Whiskey Rebellion of 1791 to 1794 over a new levy on alcoholic beverages; and battles with Native Americans and Indigenous populations over the U.S. westward expansion.

Legislators passed this bill to allow presidents to deploy state or national military forces as needed and without any authorization from Congress. All the chief executive required was to conclude that there were "unlawful obstructions, combinations, or assemblages, or rebellion against the authority of the United States." Once any of those conditions were met, the president could "call into Federal service such of the militia of any State, and use such of the armed forces, as he considers necessary to enforce those laws or to suppress the rebellion."[15]

The problem here is the undefined character of the rationale used to invoke military forces and the unilateral nature of the power. Presidents could utilize the excuse of street protests or public riots to deploy state or federal troops and effectively take control of targeted areas. That could be individual neighborhoods, cities, or states, depending on the breadth of the disturbances. The lack of meaningful limits on executive authority creates the possibility of serious abuses of power and threats to civil liberties.

Second, in more recent decades, Congress has enacted a series of emergency declaration laws that allow presidents to act unilaterally for an extended period of time. The idea is that in a modern world, disasters can unfold, emergencies can erupt, or problems can arise that require immediate action. Rather than wait on legislative or agency approval, which can take time, lawmakers empowered chief executives to deal with a variety of problems based on that individual's own predilections.

Researcher Elizabeth Goitein of the Brennan Center for Justice has documented 123 areas where presidents currently have these kinds of powers.[16] For example, after declaring a "national emergency" on a largely unconstrained basis, the leader can freeze financial accounts, launch foreign attacks, restrict border entries, shut down communications, requisition private ships, take over facilities necessary for national defense, impose trade tariffs, call up the National Guard, or undertake a whole host of other actions across the country. The sheer number of domains where the president has extraordinary power is frightening, and in the wrong hands, could result in undemocratic actions.

Concerned about possible abuses following the Richard Nixon administration, in 1976, Congress passed the National Emergencies Act to impose some limitations on these powers. Yet that legislation requires only that the chief executive "specify in the declaration which powers he intends to use, issue public updates if he decides to invoke additional powers, and report to Congress on the government's emergency-related expenditures every six months."[17] Those are not meaningful limitations on what presidents can do, and, like the Insurrection Act, they could be subject to considerable misuse.

Third, lawmakers can place partisan restrictions on voting. Indeed, during 2021, a number of states actually passed legislation that reduced the power of local election authorities and secretaries of state to assess cases of vote fraud allegations and increased the ability of state legislatures to resolve electoral disputes and choose electors for the Electoral College, even independently of the popular vote.[18] According to the Brennan Center for Justice, Republicans during 2021 introduced 389 bills in 48 states designed to increase state legislative power over elections.[19] The legislation allows local election board members to be removed from office, encourages more balloting audits and inspections, and in some places reduces the number of polling places in minority neighborhoods, among other actions.[20]

These bills are clearly problematic from the standpoints of electoral fairness and equity.[21] They target populations known to vote in particular ways and create barriers that harm specific parties. They advantage the party controlling the state legislature and enable leaders to engage in unfair lawmaking. Because most African Americans lean Democratic, Republican lawmakers enacted restrictions to make it harder for those individuals to vote, knowing that such diminutions will benefit the GOP politically and help them stay in power.[22]

Despite rather obvious biases in the impact of these bills, the U.S. Supreme Court has shown little inclination to invalidate voting restrictions that hurt African Americans and Latinos. In several cases, a majority of justices has gutted federal oversight of state voting laws, removed major enforcement powers, and allowed state legislatures to implement restrictions known to have unfair impacts on minority voters.[23]

These rulings are in addition to other court decisions that allow partisan gerrymandering of legislative districts and large amounts of secret contributions (so-called dark money) to dominate elections and governance. Taken together, these decisions weaken governance because they tilt political activity in favor of a specific party (the GOP) and limit the transparency of large donors in politics.

Finally, the Electoral Count Act is worrisome because it remains to this day the chief law designed to deal with contested elections. It had been enacted in 1887 following the disputed 1876 race. In that campaign, Democrat Samuel Tilden defeated Republican Rutherford Hayes in the popular vote, but there had been allegations of ballot fraud in Florida, Louisiana, and South Carolina (plus one disputed elector in Oregon), which meant that neither candidate got a majority in the Electoral College. To resolve the ballot disputes, Congress formed a fifteen-person Electoral Commission comprising five House members, five senators, and five Supreme Court justices. After reviewing the evidence, the Commission voted 8–7 along party lines to award the disputed electors to Hayes, which allowed him to defeat Tilden in the Electoral College on a razor thin 185 to 184 vote.[24]

In return for winning the presidency, Hayes agreed to withdraw federal troops from the South, where they had been since the Civil War. Their mission had been to enforce the peace, stop violence directed at African Americans, and ensure compliance with new voting rights, equality under the law, and the abolition of slavery, which had been added to the Constitution. That fateful decision to withdraw military forces enabled white Southern leaders to engage in vigilante violence against African Americans, suppress the minority vote, and regain political control of their states.[25]

It was a partisan deal that robbed minority residents of their political and economic rights that had briefly been gained following the war. It would take almost a century until Congress enacted new civil rights and voting rights rules in 1964 and 1965 that restored some equity in the political process and reduced the voting barriers that had marginalized minority residents. The end of Southern Reconstruction through a contested election was a clear indication of the tragic human, political, and policy consequences that resulted from contentious campaigns and failed democratic procedures.

A decade after the 1876 race, Congress enacted the Electoral Control Act to clarify vote counting and certification. Yet the legislation is vague and filled with contradictions and loopholes that can be exploited by unprincipled politicians. The bill established a long and complicated process that delegated most influence to the states in terms of vote certification. Local election boards would tabulate the ballots, and the results had to be certified either by the governor or secretary of state, depending on state law.

However, if competing slates of electors are sent to Congress by particular states, it remains up to that body to resolve ballot disputes and determine which party's slate gets accepted. It takes only one House member and one senator to object to a state's vote certification in order to invoke a congressional debate and vote on the contested electors. It is then the job of the vice president presiding over the Senate to accept the final vote certification.[26]

One Trump sympathizer argued that the vice president had the independent authority to certify the vote however he or she wanted. Attorney John Eastman authored a controversial opinion in what came to be known as the "coup memo," which sought to persuade Vice President Mike Pence to nullify Biden's victory and name Trump the presidential winner.[27] According to the lawyer, allegations of vote fraud allowed Pence to reject state electors he thought were tainted and to certify his own party's electors. Although Pence rejected that argument after talking to his own legal advisers, the episode demonstrates that there are plenty of ways state legislators, members of Congress, and the vice president can create undemocratic mischief via the ascertainment and certification processes.

Poisonous Atmosphere

Amid all these worrisome developments, substantial parts of middle America are siding with former president Trump. They accept his dishonest claim about a stolen election and view Democrats as leading the country toward socialism and bankruptcy. Indeed, according to 2021 polling by the University of Virginia, "A strong majority of Trump voters see no real difference between Democrats and socialists."[28] Rather than stand up to the former president and move the party in a different direction, congressional Republicans support Trump's lies, and allies in crucial states have passed legislation designed to weaken voter referenda, empower poll watchers, punish protesters, and allow state legislatures to overturn the popular vote in future presidential races.[29]

As a native of the U.S. heartland, I was not surprised at these shifts because most of my high school friends where I grew up in rural Ohio stand with former President Trump and express their deep reservations in communications over social media about what they see as unfair actions by opponents. They believe Antifa forces were responsible for the January 6th violence and feel liberals are traitorous hypocrites who no longer love the country. They feel that those living on the coasts do not understand middle America and want to move the country in a dangerous direction.

One of my old friends posted a message warning that liberals were pushing the United States toward communism and that in the aftermath of the contentious election, Trump should consider the imposition of martial law in order to stay in power. The fraud was so widespread, this person argued, that extraconstitutional means were warranted.

In December 2020, former Trump's national security advisor, Michael Flynn, advocated this extraordinary approach when he urged Trump to rerun the election in parts of the country due to voting fraud. He said the then president "could order, within the swing states, if he wanted to, he could take military capabilities, and he could place those in states and basically rerun an election in each of those states. I mean it's not unprecedented. These people are out there talking about martial law like it's something that we've never done. Martial law has been instituted 64 times."[30]

That and other statements from prominent conservatives inflamed what was already a tense situation. A couple of months later, after I published a picture of the Capitol building still standing, another friend from my youth directed a more ominous warning my way: "It is really too bad that you are a member of a party of cheaters and communists. Wishing you the best and hoping for a day of reckoning for your party."

On social media platforms, old friends complained about the capital city's "cockroaches" and said it was time to use the popular bugkiller Raid to get rid of political adversaries. I was not sure whether they were aware of the loaded language they were using. The first time I had heard that term had been in regard to the 1994 Rwandan Civil War, when members of the Hutu tribe used the language to dehumanize their ethnic rivals and justify their brutal murders of a million Tutsies.

These chilling exchanges by past acquaintances made me wonder whether America was on the precipice of an all-out conflict. Would the societal antagonism get out of hand and escalate to an even more dangerous degree? Would America move toward being an authoritarian state that would root out opponents and thought leaders in a way that had happened in other countries? How would academic experts and friends of democracy survive the deteriorating environment concerning truth, reason, and logic? Those of us who write about American politics and public policy sit in the crosshairs of an intense polarization, and it is not easy to navigate the tumultuous wake of the sharp national divide.

Risks for Civil Society

Think tanks, universities, nonprofits, and the knowledge sector in general represent an important prism for all this political turmoil as the experts who work in academic organizations are prime targets for those who mistrust privileged elites and believe the country has veered off in the wrong direction. What is happening with those entities is a sign of much deeper maladies afflicting the body politic.

In his 2021 book, *What Universities Owe Democracy*, Johns Hopkins University president Ronald Daniels argues that "the fates of democracy and universities are intertwined." He notes the rising threat of authoritarianism in the United States and around the world and writes that "independent universities unnerve authoritarians because everything that these institutions strive to achieve is inimical to the autocrat's devotion to the accumulation and arbitrary exercise of coercive public power."[31] Illiberal leaders prefer misinformation, disinformation, and conspiracy theories over facts and reason because the former allow them to create alternative realities and fake information that favors the dictator's personal whims and political predilections. Facts constrain autocrats in ways nearly all of them dislike. They crave the exercise of raw political power over reason-based deliberation and fact-based analysis.

As the United States shows worrisome signs of the utilization of fear and emotion over facts and reason, the political atmosphere is poisonous for academic experts who operate on the basis of logic. In the think tank area and the world of higher education, scholars pride themselves on their ability to analyze problems and generate workable solutions, and leaders count on their help in making public policy.

Yet increasingly, their analysis is under attack from those who mistrust expertise and want to discredit their work. They believe many things researchers do are partisan, extreme, or corrupt. Leaders today regularly challenge basic truths and do not accept the conclusions of leading thinkers and scientists.

We see that tendency among climate skeptics, antivaxxers, people who fervently believe the 2020 election was stolen from Trump, and those who think antifascist elements known as Antifa or the FBI falsely framed Trump supporters for the January 6 U.S. Capitol insurrection. Holding erroneous viewpoints or perspectives entirely at odds with accepted scientific evidence is no longer rare.

As Harvard professor Thomas Patterson notes in his book, *How America Lost Its Mind: The Assault on Reason That's Crippling Our Democracy*, there is a "slow-motion" destruction that is threatening U.S. democracy.[32] A gradual disintegration of respect for the truth is threatening our political system as "alternative facts" tear the country apart and fuel a dangerous polarization. Each side has its own realities, which makes bargaining, compromise, and negotiation virtually impossible.

If U.S. democracy falters, as prominent academics have warned, the undermining of progress will become acute. There are risky shifts taking place in media coverage, information transmission, voting rights, congressional oversight, judicial impartiality, and civil liberties that endanger the future. People should no longer assume that due process will safeguard their procedural rights or that the court of public opinion will root out the worst abuses in civic life. There is no invisible hand that guarantees the future of American democracy.

Political scientists Steven Livingston and W. Lance Bennett argue that an attack on "authoritative institutions" fuels misinformation and makes it possible for false and undemocratic material to spread broadly over social media. Once key substantive gatekeepers are discredited, it becomes easy for partisan politicians and slanted media sites to challenge shared realities, spread propaganda, rile up supporters, and attack real or perceived opponents.[33] They point out how wealthy donors have funded nonprofits, think tanks, and advocacy organizations in ways that undermine science, news organizations, and civic dialogue.[34]

It is time to step back from this dangerous precipice, analyze what is happening, and discuss why these developments represent serious threats to American democracy, procedural justice, the scientific establishment, and a reason-based society. There are no guarantees that facts will triumph over falsehoods and reason will dominate over emotion. Power politics and authoritarianism are gaining strength not just in the United States but around the globe, and there are signs of a "might makes right" mentality among political leaders. In a world dominated by fear, anger, and grievance, we have to seriously doubt whether the long arc of history will bend toward justice, liberty, and freedom.

3

The Changing Political and Media Landscape

Several years ago, I wrote a Brookings book entitled *Megachange: Economic Disruption, Political Upheaval, and Social Strife in the 21st Century.*[1] In it, I argued that we live in a time of large-scale transformation that is upending many aspects of contemporary life. Both the pace and the scope of change are accelerating, and the swiftness of the transformation poses many challenges for society, politics, and the economy.

In a very short period of time, the current environment has changed radically for the worse. Social media tools such as Facebook, Instagram, YouTube, Twitter, and others provide public platforms for personal attacks, extremist rhetoric, false statements, and polarized behavior. Domestic politics has become tribal, and adversaries are seen as enemies. The venom that is prevalent in civic discourse is both worrisome and dangerous.[2]

At the same time, large-scale alterations have raised people's anxieties. Climate shifts are producing wildfires, drought, floods, and extreme weather events. Income inequality is high and is limiting opportunities for economic advancement. Technological changes are disrupting whole industries and creating widespread fears about job losses, misinformation, data breaches, and a loss of confidential information. Racial injustice and gender inequality persist in ways that threaten the very fabric of society. COVID-19 challenged our public health infrastructure and led many to doubt the health recommendations of medical experts.

And internationally, there are shifts that have destabilized traditional alignments and spread false information around the world. China, Iran, North Korea, Russia, Saudi Arabia, Turkey, and others are expanding their activities and complicating the geopolitical situation. There are tensions with long-term allies, and relations with adversaries have become fraught with risk. Unless one is very careful, it is easy to step on proverbial landmines in the international arena that will blow you apart.

It is a difficult environment at virtually every level. Public opinion surveys show people worrying that the overall pace of change is taking place too quickly, and they are having difficulties coping with the tremendous shifts.[3] Anxiety is high, and people wonder what all the alterations will mean for them politically, economically, personally, and socially. It is a period that is testing the faith, determination, and dedication of all involved, while creating opportunities to destabilize society and disrupt governance.

Weaponization of Information

In the current period, people from many different organizations face political or legal risks from expressing their personal viewpoints. Academic freedom is under attack and time-worn protections based on freedom of speech or freedom of the press have started to unravel. Reporters, legislators, and administration officials have been investigated for leaks, and those who write critical commentaries about public people have become the subject of defamation lawsuits.

Recognizing the shifting legal landscape, Trump made a practice during his time in office of weaponizing libel and defamation laws by suing op-ed authors who wrote opinion pieces critical of him. In 2020, for example, his campaign lawyers filed lawsuits against writers for the *New York Times*, *Washington Post*, and CNN. The suits claimed op-ed articles had impugned Trump's character by claiming that there was a quid pro quo between Russia and the billionaire to aid his 2016 election. The article in the *Times* was written by former executive editor Max Frankel, who argued that there was a "quid of help in the campaign against Hillary Clinton for the quo of a new pro-Russian foreign policy."[4]

In addition, according to Trump's attorneys, the *Post*'s columns by Greg Sargent and Paul Waldman cited false and defamatory arguments suggesting a Russian conspiracy to help candidate Trump.[5] The CNN article was written by Larry Noble, a former member of the Federal Election Commission, who said Trump was open to Russian assistance.[6]

Months later, many of these suits were dismissed by judges on grounds that they lacked merit, but their mere filing ran up legal fees and contributed to an atmosphere of fear and intimidation in many quarters.[7] Writers had to worry that if they authored pieces critical of the president or other people, their personal texts and emails would be subpoenaed, their phone calls would be monitored, or they would be sued and forced to spend a lot of money defending themselves.

To add teeth to people's fears, Trump officials filed subpoenas to get the phone and email records of leading broadcasters, newspaper reporters, members of Congress, and even his own White House staff. Overall, seventy-three phone numbers and thirty-six email addresses were investigated over several years.[8] Using the U.S. Department of Justice, administrators sought these records in order to determine who was leaking material to the press. As part of this investigation, more than a dozen members of Congress and staffers on the House Intelligence Committee had their personal information revealed to prosecutors looking for damaging material. Even though little incriminating evidence was found, it was a sign of how far the administration was willing to go to investigate opponents and direct the tremendous power of government against critics.[9]

Some of the criticisms levied against news reporters even had actual physical consequences. An analysis by the Radio Television Digital News Directors Association in 2021 found that 20 percent of TV news directors said their television staff was attacked while filming video footage during the past year.[10] When verbal attacks on the media turn into actual violence from onlookers, we cross a dangerous point for the system as a whole.

Well-known professors are not immune from the risks of the shifting political landscape. Virginia GOP chair Rich Anderson asked the University of Virginia to investigate Professor Larry Sabato after he tweeted "Trump, who governed on the edge of insanity for four long years, has gone over the edge. Yet millions of people and 90%+ of GOP members of Congress still genuflect before this false god." The prominent commentator said this after Trump claimed in 2021 that he would be reinstated as president. Anderson made the investigation request on the grounds that the educator's statements "appear to violate the university's mission statement and faculty code of ethics" and that they represented "bitter partisanship." Fortunately, university officials defended academic freedom by putting out a statement reminding people that "there is nothing in the university's code of conduct that limits faculty from engaging in expression that is protected under the First Amendment."[11]

Similar problems popped up on other campuses. When three University of Florida election experts were asked to testify in a voting rights lawsuit regarding the detrimental impact of new election restrictions on minority voters, school officials denied them the right to apply their expertise even though expert testimony is common among professors. Governor Ron DeSantis complained that Florida university professors should not testify against a state law and college administrators agreed with that stance, thereby eliminating the ability of these academics to contribute their expertise to a matter of major public debate. As noted by reporters at the time, that "ban is an extraordinary limit on speech that raises questions of academic freedom and First Amendment rights."[12] However, the university reversed its stance when the professors sued to protect their freedom of speech.[13]

Ease of Personal Destruction

The deeply partisan contemporary environment poses many challenges. There are intense divisions between Right and Left, Republicans and Democrats, and liberals, moderates, and conservatives. Public opinion surveys undertaken by professors Shibley Telhami and Stella Rouse of the University of Maryland show tremendous differences between party groupings. When asked about their most important identities, Republicans cited their traditional religious and cultural beliefs, while Democrats focused on inequality, social justice, and seeing the world as an interconnected whole.[14]

In a polarized atmosphere, each part of society fights passionately over conflicting values, problem definitions, policy priorities, and the future of the country.[15] In this high-stakes environment, many people do not trust others, and there is a combativeness to civil discourse that inflames personal feelings and makes it impossible for leaders to address important problems. Indeed, it is hard to adjudicate "the truth" or create a common reality when personal viewpoints are diametrically opposed and everyone has their own facts.[16]

It is shockingly easy during such a time period to undermine people and institutions. There are partisan media forces and commercial firms whose mission is to find targets and spread damaging information. Sometimes, the accusations are factually accurate, while at other times they are erroneous, but still make people look bad.

As an illustration, Democratic representative Katie Hill was forced to resign her seat when, during a contentious divorce, her soon to be ex-husband is said to have provided personal text messages and nude photos of her to a conservative website called Red State. The platform published the information along with lurid stories about her bisexual lifestyle.[17]

It is an indication of the risks facing politicians who have grown up in an oversharing environment of sexting, nude selfies, and alternative lifestyles.[18] According to a study published in the *Journal of the American Medical Association Pediatrics*, one in seven young people under age eighteen have sexted explicit pictures or texts to other individuals. A number also reported forwarding such messages to other individuals without the sender's consent.[19]

As these individuals enter the workforce, their past behavior could expose them to blackmail, extortion, or revenge porn. Pictures taken on a whim could resurface years later as a lethal personal or political weapon. Colleague Quinta Jurecic notes in her article about Hill's public shaming that the episode revealed "how ugly the political landscape could become and a reminder of how ugly, for the many ordinary people who have suffered this kind of abuse, the world already is."[20]

Writing later about her own outing, Hill emphasized the toxic relationship with her husband and the risks she took when she decided to end their marriage. "It wasn't the first time I had tried to leave; the last time was less than a month before the [2018] election, and when I tried, he made it clear to me that if I left, he would ruin me," she wrote.[21] Some time after she left her husband, the nude pictures surfaced, and her promising political career was shattered. It seemed to be a dramatic example of revenge porn and a sign of the double standard prominent women face. "We have men who have been credibly accused of intentional acts of sexual violence and remain in boardrooms, on the Supreme Court, in this very body, and, worst of all in the Oval Office," Hill remarked. But she lost her legislative position over the revelation.[22]

Even for those who have done nothing unusual, there are "slander" websites and "disinformation for hire" firms that can quickly disseminate inaccurate information.[23] They take unverified online comments and spread them across a network of domains. Quickly, that information can populate search results and become among the first things the inquisitive discover about people when they look for online information. Even more disturbing, some of the web developers who operate these sites have parallel operations that charge thousands of dollars to remove this very same information, which makes for a lucrative business of "digital sliming."[24]

Sometimes, government officials provide confidential information on people in seeming violation of federal privacy protections. Democracy Forward, a nonprofit government oversight organization, documented several cases where the Trump-led Department of Homeland Security (DHS) is said to have provided conservative news organizations with confidential information about people's immigration and citizenship status. For example, when Fox News broadcast a story about an Iraq man who had shot a policeman, a DHS official emailed Alex Pappas of Fox News that the shooter was a refugee and suggested it be included in the story. In another case, DHS deputy press secretary Katie Miller informed John Binder of Breitbart News that a man accused of sexual abuse was a U.S. citizen, not an illegal immigrant.[25]

In 2021, it was revealed that an obscure unit within the U.S. Department of Commerce known as the Investigations and Threat Management Service monitored communications both inside and outside the agency. Examiners found that staffers "covertly searched employees' offices at night, ran broad keyword searches of their emails trying to surface signs of foreign influence and scoured Americans' social media for critical comments about the census." People with "ethnic surnames" or who came from "Asian and Middle Eastern descent" were targeted for special attention. Even though this spying was of questionable legality, it persisted for a considerable time until halted by the Biden administration.[26]

Vulnerabilities of Digital Technology

As the country grappled with polarized politics and a health pandemic, technology became a lifesaver for many people. In a short period of time early in 2020, many were pushed by public health circumstances into online education, telemedicine, remote work, video conferencing, and e-commerce.

But the new tools also revealed stark inequities and vulnerabilities. Not everybody has access to the high-speed broadband or mobile technology that enables digital life. Millions are being left behind, being unable to get electronic health care, take advantage of online education, work from home, or apply for jobs online.[27]

At the same time, in a world where people undertake numerous virtual activities, geolocation data, emails, and text messages can be easily compromised and made public without any warning. Data breaches are common, and there is little security in the digital world. Some cybersecurity experts joke that there are two types of organizations in the world now: those that have been hacked and know it, and those that have been compromised and don't know it.

For example, phone location information can detail people's personal movements. A conservative newsletter used geolocation data to claim a Catholic priest was visiting gay bars. Drawing on anonymized location information that then was linked to his home and work address, the newsletter publicly outed the clergyman. The priest subsequently resigned his job at the U.S. Conference of Catholic Bishops, and the episode revealed quite dramatically how we live in a digital period when supposedly confidential information is no longer secure.[28] When asked about this episode, former White House technology adviser Ashkan Soltani noted that "all of this stuff is really available out there. There is a risk for anyone who uses these apps. This could potentially happen to anyone."[29]

It was a development that author Shoshana Zuboff popularized through her notion of "surveillance capitalism." In a book, she documented the ways large technology platforms and business interests engaged in data collection, mining, and analytics and in the process threatened personal privacy and human values. The sheer volume of information generated through a wide range of digital tools put everyone at risk in ways they often did not fully understand.[30]

Another indication of virtual vulnerability came a few years ago with the hacking of Democratic adviser John Podesta's emails. He was a top adviser to presidential candidate Hillary Clinton and close friend to many influential Washingtonians. When the breach revealed his thousands of emails to prominent people throughout the country, it showed Podesta's efforts to help friends and extend his network. In an era of mass cynicism, his communiques smacked of insider dealings and confirmed many voters' views regarding the need for wholesale political change.

That hack represented a sign of rising digital exposure. Those who worked in the federal government saw their personnel files stolen in a hack of U.S. Office of Personnel and Management databases. Although it is always impossible in cybercrimes to prove culpability, security experts suspected the Chinese, who need large data sets to train their artificial intelligence and machine learning systems. Many organizations are seeing their confidential information published online or used for illicit purposes. There are tremendous cybersecurity risks because hacking a site means its sensitive documents can end up in the public domain overnight.

In 2020, an even more egregious heist took place. Russian agents utilized security patch updates from a company called SolarWinds to infiltrate numerous public and private sector organizations. The information technology systems of U.S. government departments at Defense, Treasury, Commerce, and Energy were violated as were those of leading companies, nonprofits, universities, and think tanks. The cyberinvasion took place covertly over a period of many months, and no one was sure what material had been compromised, only that the scale of the operation was massive.[31]

In 2021, China is said to have hacked Enterprise Email systems at over 30,000 U.S. organizations. Government officials described the breach as "very, very serious" and noted that businesses, state and federal agencies, universities, think tanks, and nonprofit groups were infiltrated.[32] The latter comment concerned many in the nonprofit world since a number of organizations used enterprise software.

Then an East Coast energy transit run by Colonial Pipeline was sabotaged in an act of ransomware, where the infiltrators digitally shut down computer systems and demanded payment to remove the malware and restore system operability. It was an egregious attack that slowed fuel delivery to much of the East Coast of the United States for several days until the company paid $4.4 million to a criminal enterprise called DarkSide that operated out of Russia and Eastern Europe.[33] For awhile before pumping resumed, there were long lines at service stations in a number of U.S. cities as residents dealt with the gasoline shortages.

Large, globally oriented organizations weren't spared from the risk of cybersecurity incursions. In the middle of the coronavirus pandemic, the World Health Organization, National Institutes of Health, World Bank, Centers for Disease Control and Prevention, Wuhan Institute of Virology, and Gates Foundation saw their internal databases breached. Email addresses along with confidential passwords were published online via 4chan, a platform for extremist groups. Thieves claimed the attack represented a way to express discontent with the handling of the virus and for "the far right to weaponize the COVID-19 pandemic." Around 25,000 addresses were exposed to those on the political edge as a vehicle to harass global elites.[34]

Even the most powerful people in our society are unable to protect themselves from hacks and leaks. Salacious texts and pictures from Amazon CEO Jeff Bezos to his girlfriend, Lauren Sanchez, were exposed by the *National Enquirer*. The news leak ended his twenty-five-year marriage to MacKenzie Bezos and led to a $38 billion divorce settlement, making it the most costly personal data breach in human history. The hack led to a plethora of negative news stories about the wealthy man and besmirched his reputation.

Investigating the source of the leak, a forensic study commissioned by Bezos found that Saudi Crown Prince Mohammed bin Salman had retaliated against the owner of the *Washington Post* for the newspaper's critical coverage of the royal's involvement in the gruesome 2018 death of Saudi critic, Jamal Khashoggi. After meeting Bezos at a Los Angeles dinner and getting his phone number, bin Salman sent the billionaire a WhatsApp message with an MP4 video promoting Saudi Arabia's economy. Unbeknownst to Bezos, the study claimed a file contained surveillance software that surreptitiously delivered his private texts and pictures to Saudi authorities.[35] Others, though, cited a more pedestrian source of the media leak. A *Bloomberg Businessweek* article argued that the texts and pictures came from Sanchez's brother, who got the information from his sister and sold the material to the *Enquirer* for $200,000.[36]

Bill Gates was not hacked, but he underwent negative press scrutiny based on leaked emails regarding his ties to convicted sex offender Jeffrey Epstein and other alleged personal misbehaviors. Epstein, a flamboyant New York financial adviser, liked young women and held dinners, parties, and receptions where prominent men met people in his social circle. Eventually, Epstein would be found guilty of having sex with underage girls and exploiting them for his own purposes. He would ultimately kill himself in prison.

While the exact scope of Gates's connection with Epstein remains unclear, news stories report that he spent late nights at the Epstein mansion, held many meetings with him, flew on his plane, discussed joint ventures with him, and received philanthropic advice from him. In one email leaked to journalists, Gates described Epstein in the following terms: "His lifestyle is very different and kind of intriguing although it would not work for me." In other correspondence sent to a colleague, Gates admired Epstein's charm and noted a meeting where "a very attractive Swedish woman and her daughter dropped by and I ended up staying there quite late." Ultimately, that and other behaviors were cited in Bill Gates's divorce from Melinda French Gates in 2021, making it a rather expensive privacy breach for the billionaire.[37]

Disclosures to the *Wall Street Journal* furthermore revealed that Gates had an inappropriate affair with a Microsoft employee while serving on the company's board. Amid claims of harassment and discrimination from other staffers, the firm commissioned a formal investigation into the matter, but Gates resigned from the Microsoft board before a report was finished. His spokesperson admitted to the *Journal* that "there was an affair almost 20 years ago which ended amicably."[38] Around the same time, the *New York Times* reported that Gates "had a pattern of courting women in the workplace" that made some of his subordinates uncomfortable with him.[39]

These episodes involving bad behavior by two of the wealthiest men in America reveal how the threat of personal exposure lurks beneath the surface of twenty-first-century life. Newspaper columnists pointed out that "If Bezos Can Get Hacked, You Can Too." Writer Paul Sullivan noted the ominous threats facing regular people in a *New York Times* column. "In the last two years, security experts have seen a steady increase in simple schemes to get into accounts, like phishing, as well as more complicated campaigns to gain control over a victim's financial life, like taking over a phone or a computer." The columnist advised people not to discuss their vacations on social media, not to use free wi-fi in hotels and restaurants, and to understand the risks of manufactured "deepfake" videos that falsely put people in compromising positions or showed them making controversial statements they actually had not made.[40]

It was a lesson not lost on me or anyone else. Virtually every day at Brookings, I received phishing attacks designed to compromise my emails or unlock my bank account. There were messages about undelivered packages, email services that were about to be terminated unless I logged onto my account, unpaid invoices, speaking invitations, and many other creative scams. When that failed, the potential infiltrators switched to text messages and told me I was about to be charged $799 unless I went to a link that would remove the charge from my credit card. Regularly, I worried about clicking on the wrong thing and seeing my business messages or financial material published on the internet.

Challenges of the Trump Era

Sensitivities surrounding technology, though, are less worrisome compared to the political rancor unleashed during the Trump presidency. Elected in 2016, he quickly violated long-established norms of democratic governance based on executive actions, administrative practices, and congressional oversight. He was openly rude to opponents and castigated anyone who criticized him. He made insensitive remarks regarding race, gender, and immigration. And in terms of foreign policy, he antagonized allies and cozied up to authoritarian rulers.[41]

By 2019, Democrats were confronted with what they saw as sufficient evidence of wrongdoing and the House of Representatives moved toward impeachment. In sympathy with this action, some Brookings scholars openly called for his removal from office as they were alarmed by the fact that during a phone call with the Ukrainian president, Trump had asked his counterpart to investigate his leading Democratic rival, Joe Biden, in an effort to sabotage his candidacy, and he threatened to withhold needed U.S. military funding in that nation's battle against Russia if President Volodymyr Zelensky did not publicly announce an investigation.

Ultimately, the power machinations caught up to the president. Trump's initial impeachment took place at a time when everything in D.C. was polarized. It riveted the country as people debated the appropriateness of the investigation and whether he should be removed from office. Supporters describe the effort as a witch hunt while others saw Trump's various activities as a clear threat to the Constitution and the rule of law.

Trump and his allies in the media, business, and government

challenged civil society in ways that were quite alarming. He would rant about fake news, complain about liberal professors, criticize think tanks, attack nonprofits, promote unfounded conspiracy theories, and undermine independent fact-checkers. Anyone who was in a position to challenge his inaccuracies was subject to personal attacks, either from Trump himself or from those who mimicked his criticisms.

Big Lies and Conspiracy Theories

In an effort to undermine Biden, virtually every day between the 2020 election and 2021 inauguration, Trump complained about ballot fraud and a "rigged election," and most Republicans across the country agreed that there had been widespread fraud.[42] Later, he would call it the crime of the century.

His allies campaigned on the slogan of "stop the steal" and argued that mail ballots had been abused by Democrats in large enough numbers to tilt the campaign away from the chief executive. Lawsuits were filed alleging massive election fraud, and the case reached the Supreme Court. One of my proudest moments came when an amicus brief filed by state attorneys general cited my policy paper arguing that there had not been meaningful fraud and that military personnel had voted by mail for years without any corruption or controversy.[43]

In pursuing this strategy, conservatives are following an approach that Brookings scholar Jonathan Rauch says draws on a notion popularized by Breitbart News chairman and later Trump adviser Steve Bannon of "flood the zone with shit." The idea is to spread so much misinformation and disinformation that it becomes impossible to discern the truth and easy to believe that at least some of it actually is true.[44] It is a perspective that authoritarian leaders love to practice to great effect. All you have to do is deploy "shit-posters" and "shitlords" whose job is to disseminate false information, wait for the lies to spread widely, and use propaganda to blur the truth, get people mad, and keep them angry.

Once Trump's lies were broadly disseminated, Republican legislators acted on those falsehoods, cracked down on voting rights, and retaliated against GOP leaders such as Representative Liz Cheney, who condemned the blatant misinformation. Election experts feared the numerous ways in which democracy was being undermined. Significant limits were placed on voting rights even though there was no meaningful evidence of ballot fraud.

Based on this and other actions, observers worried whether America was witnessing the rise of a "post-fact" world. In a highly partisan era, it was hard to find objective perspectives and easy to promote what were called "alternative facts."[45] Clear falsehoods circulated as readily as long-accepted truths. Writers Naomi Oreskes and Erik Conway use the controversies over the health consequences of tobacco smoking and the environmental ramifications of climate change to talk about how "merchants of doubt" intentionally obscure the facts. They note how a few scientists financed by industry peddled junk science and led some people to doubt the dangers of smoking or the risks of climate change, and how damaging this was for civic discourse.[46]

Perils during the Biden Presidency

Trump's 2020 election defeat did not ease the major threats to think tanks, nonprofits, news organizations, and opinion leaders. Within a month of Election Day, the *New York Times* ran a front page story alleging conflicts of interest among Biden administration appointments.[47] After departing the Obama administration, several top advisers had taken jobs with or given talks to consulting firms or investment companies. The story frowned on these moves and cited progressive Democrats who were upset that these individuals had provided advice to leading military contractors or given speeches to financial institutions. It was a sign that outside scrutiny and public cynicism were not going to subside even with the departure of President Trump, and that there would be high-profile attacks on administration officials.

One of Joe Biden's nominees to head the Office of Management and Budget was Neera Tanden, who was president of the liberal think tank Center for American Progress. She directed an institution that had championed progressive ideas designed to fight income inequality, mitigate climate change, raise taxes on the wealthy, and fight for human rights around the world. She was a skilled advocate with a long history of progressive activism.

Yet shortly after her nomination was announced, the *Washington Post* ran a critical investigative story complaining that she led "a think tank backed by corporate and foreign interests."[48] Tanden's think tank openly listed its donors on its website, and the article noted its money came from private equity, financial firms, technology companies, health care providers, and foreign governments. The article quoted critics such as Matt Bruenig of the People's Policy Project saying, "Neera Tanden has spent the last decade raising money from the top companies and highest-net-worth individuals in the country, which is a bit at odds with what Biden pitched during the campaign." The reporters claimed that this and other think tanks acted as "unregistered lobbyists," engaged in "influence laundering," and had close ties with authoritarian governments, such as Saudi Arabia and the United Arab Emirates.

Ironically, though, it wasn't fundraising but tweeting that doomed her nomination. A number of senators objected to acerbic posts she had written about their colleagues. For example, she said Senator Susan Collins of Maine was "the worst" and that "vampires have 'more heart' than Sen. Ted Cruz."[49] Even more problematic was a 2016 tweet criticizing Mylan CEO Heather Bresch as she was the daughter of crucial Senate swing voter Joe Manchin.[50] Although some of Trump's nominees had done far worse things on Twitter, Tanden was forced to withdraw when Manchin announced his opposition and no Republican senator would support her appointment. In a 50-50 Senate, Manchin undoubtably relished the personal payback given Tanden's verbal affront to his daughter.

Even after Trump departed the scene, there continued to be attacks on the news media, think tank experts, and nonprofit organizations from the right-wing outrage industry. Republicans saw the idea of a stolen election as their route back to power, and many of them repeated blatant falsehoods across the country. Conservative television, newspaper, radio, and internet sites promoted those claims even though there was no factual basis for them, and public opinion surveys showed most Republicans continued to believe the lies.[51]

Within GOP circles, Biden and the people who worked for him were portrayed as illegitimate, dishonest, partisan, and corrupt. While many thought Biden was doing a good job, a significant number opposed him and questioned the legitimacy of his election. Anything that undermined administration staffers or external sympathizers was seen as good for the opposition party's prospects.

The political scene was set for chaotic battles over the future of the country, and think tanks, universities, and nonprofit organizations would be right in the middle of those controversies. It would prove surprisingly simple to challenge scientific and academic expertise. At a time when many Americans were suspicious of liberal professors, D.C.-based think tanks, and scientific consensus on matters of election fraud, climate change, vaccinations, and mask wearing, it would be easy for politicians to sow public mistrust and discord and to claim that experts were charlatans who shouldn't be taken seriously.[52]

4

Public Opinion

The political climate in the United States is risky due to the wide fissures among citizens and leaders. Enabled by volatile social media, partisan news sites, and societal disagreements over basic values, national polls reveal a population that is divided, mistrusting, intolerant, and in some cases, willing to support undemocratic actions. It is a toxic concoction that bodes poorly for our future ability to address problems and function effectively.

In addition, moderate politicians have lost their legislative seats as a result of shifts in public opinion, and this has led to the rise of more extreme leaders and members of Congress. This means the officials who used to restrain conflict and negotiate with the other party have disappeared, and the system has lost valuable guardrails that used to keep things from getting out of control.

The emergence of so many dysfunctional features has been fueled by many different developments: geographic disparities, racial injustice, demographic shifts, and governance problems; leaders who seek political advantage through polarization and extremism; a rapidly changing global situation that creates anxiety, uncertainty, and anger; and the rise of an "outrage industry" that profits from public dissatisfaction, inflammatory social media, and sensationalistic media coverage.[1]

The result is a volatile combination for all involved. Lack of support for basic elements of American democracy has already led to the adoption of policies that suppress voting rights, fuel intolerance, and create an institutional means for small groups of people to thwart the will of the majority. If continued, those actions will likely destabilize the country and generate significant social and political instability. That, in turn, could increase calls for police crackdowns and tough law enforcement to restore peace.

Divided Public

Political divisions are rampant in the contemporary period as the public is sharply divided along party lines. Table 4-1 shows substantial gaps between Republicans and Democrats on a range of major issues. The latter, for example, are much more likely than the former to believe that states can prohibit in-person religious gatherings during a pandemic, to believe that voters should be able to allow others to deliver their ballots, to think that the Affordable Care Act mandate is constitutional, and to say that it is legal to allow foster children to be placed with same-sex couples. On most of these issues, there was a gap of 30 to 40 percentage points in the views of the two parties.[2]

Supporters of each party take diametrically opposed views on most political issues, and there is a startling degree of intensity in these divisions. People differ both in the direction and the strength of their viewpoints, and those gaps make it difficult to negotiate differences and reach policy accommodations that satisfy each side.

But it is not just politics; people are divided based on lifestyle, income, education, race, and a host of other dimensions. Polarization has become deeply rooted not only in the body politic but in peo-

TABLE 4-1. Views of Democrats, Independents, and Republicans on Major Issues, 2021

	Democrats (%)	Independents (%)	Republicans (%)
States [during a pandemic] can prohibit in-person religious gatherings despite the First Amendment right to free exercise of religion	71	40	24
Voters should be able to rely on another person to collect and drop off ballots	70	46	27
The individual Affordable Care Act mandate is a tax and is constitutional	62	40	26
Requiring religious agencies to allow foster children to be placed with same-sex couples does not violate their First Amendment rights	61	43	35

Source: Stephen Jessee, Neil Malhotra, and Maya Sen, National Survey of 2,158 American adults undertaken by YouGov between April 7 and 16, 2021.

ple's restaurant choices, magazine subscriptions, television viewing habits, and sporting preferences. Marketers claim that they can determine someone's party and ideological position if they know just a few things about people's day-to-day lives. In a number of ways, people have sorted themselves into demonstrable strata across a wide variety of social, political, economic, and cultural dimensions. Given that reality, it becomes hard to bring them together behind common goals and purposes.

Lack of Public Trust

Trust in the federal government has dropped precipitously over the past decades. In 1958, figure 4-1 shows that 73 percent of Americans indicated that they trusted government to do what is right much of the time. But this number dropped to 36 percent in 1974 during the Watergate scandal involving President Richard Nixon and 21 percent in 1994 during the contentiousness of the Clinton administration. It rose to 56 percent in 2002 when the 9/11 terrorist attacks temporarily united the country. However, it fell back to 22 percent in 2012 in the aftermath of the Great Recession and dropped even further to 20 percent in 2017 and 2020 during the Trump administration.[3]

Most voters no longer trust government officials to do what is right for the general public. Instead, many think leaders are out for themselves or to serve private interests. During the periods of decline, factors such as weak economic performance, international setbacks, or domestic scandals tarnished the reputation of officeholders. This long-term shift has made it easier to play to public cynicism and to convince voters that many parts of the D.C. establishment are corrupt and unethical.

FIGURE 4-1. Trust in the Federal Government to Do What Is Right, 1958–2020

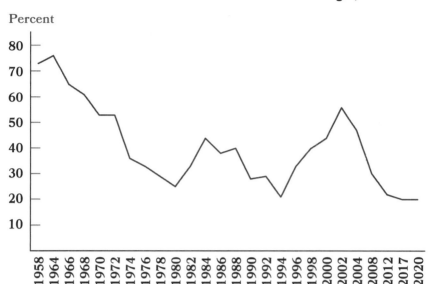

Percent

Source: For 1958 to 2012 data, University of Michigan, "Trust the Federal Government," ANES (American National Election Studies) Guide to Public Opinion and Electoral Behavior, 2014, and for 2017 to 2020 data, Pew Research Center, "Public Trust in Government," May 17, 2021.

Intolerance for the Opposition

With the growth of polarization and extremism and a lack of trust in the political system, many individuals are intolerant of those who hold different viewpoints. They don't believe that opponents are well intentioned or have the best interests of the country at heart. A number worry that the Right will drive America into authoritarianism, and the Left will move the country toward socialism.

At the same time, there is great concern about what opposition political forces will do once they are in power. A 2020 survey by the Pew Research Center, for instance, demonstrated considerable worry among the electorate. When asked if they feared the election of the opposite candidate would lead to lasting harm to the United

States, 90 percent of Biden supporters and 89 percent of Trump supporters stated that they were very concerned that election of the opposition leader would destabilize the country and create irreparable harm.

The policy disagreements between the two sides as well as the contrast in values and worldviews generate considerable consternation among voters.[4] The nation has shifted to a place where there are two tribes that vie with one another and engage in all-out attacks on those who hold different perspectives. They don't like the competing tribe, feel the other side does not have the country's best interests at heart, and are willing to fight with everything they have to defeat the opposition.

Non-democracy Support

The current configuration is a formula for a divided country with each side willing to confront the other side and in some cases consider extralegal means to contest politics and win elections. After all, lack of trust in your foes can open the door to unconventional means to gain triumph, cement your own power, and protect your personal values.

According to the 2018 American Institutional Confidence poll of 5,400 adults, only 40 percent of Americans are satisfied with U.S. democracy. A number have lost faith in democratic processes and believe things have deteriorated to the point where extraordinary steps are warranted. They don't have confidence in political leaders and think the system is rigged against people like themselves.

More worrisome, though, are the differences by age in support for democracy. Figure 4-2 breaks down views on whether "democracy is always preferable" and finds older people aged 64 or older (84 percent) are far more likely to agree with that proposition than younger people between 18 and 29 years of age (55 percent).[5] The younger someone is, the less they prefer a democratic political system.

FIGURE 4-2. U.S. Preferences for Democracy
or Non-democracies by Age, 2018

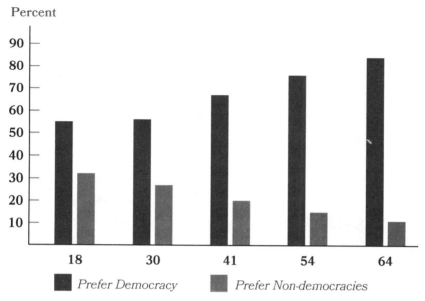

Source: Sean Kates, Jonathan Ladd, and Joshua Tucker, "Should You Worry about American Democracy?" *Washington Post,* October 24, 2018.

At the same time, younger individuals (32 percent) are more likely than older individuals (11 percent) to say "non-democracies can be preferable." They like the action orientation of those systems and the lack of institutional gridlock and paralysis that sometimes characterizes the American system. They think that authoritarian countries deliver results and are more orderly in their approach.

If those kinds of breakdowns persist as people age, the future continuation of democracy is at risk. The idea that nearly a third of young Americans are open to nondemocratic systems is disturbing, especially in light of the problematic U.S. trends already noted. A number of these individuals feel that democracies are floundering, not protecting basic values, or failing to promote economic opportunity for people.

Other national surveys document serious warning signs for

the United States. A CBS News/YouGov survey found that only 29 percent of U.S. citizens say American democracy is secure, and 71 percent think it is threatened. In addition, the same poll revealed that over half (51 percent) believe that political violence in the next few years will increase. When asked to identify the biggest threat to America's way of life, 54 percent cited "other people in America," followed by economic forces (20 percent); natural disasters or viruses (17 percent); and foreign threats (8 percent).[6]

A 2021 survey undertaken by CNN found similar results. When asked whether American democracy is under attack, 56 percent said it was, and 51 percent worried that "elected officials in the U.S. will successfully overturn the results of a future election because their party did not win." Another question revealed that "58 percent say that changes to voting laws in states controlled by Republicans were made in order to help the party in power rather than to make elections more fair."[7]

Even more ominous was the significant support for the use of political violence in the United States. In a 2021 American Values national survey undertaken by the Public Religion Research Institute, 18 percent of people across the country supported the statement that "because things have gotten so far off track, true American patriots may have to resort to violence in order to save our country." Thirty percent of Republicans agreed with that sentiment as did 26 percent of evangelical Protestants.[8]

Prevalence of Authoritarianism

As a sign of the impending crisis, several researchers have identified discernible evidence of authoritarianism in the United States. That is a perspective indicated by support for "strong-man" leaders, a high need for order, favoring traditional cultural values, engaging in racial bigotry, fearing diversity, having a willingness to suppress dissidents, and demonstrating a lack of regard for democratic elections and procedural safeguards.

According to writer Matthew MacWilliams, "Roughly 40 percent of Americans tend to favor authority, obedience and uniformity over freedom, independence and diversity." He notes that authoritarianism is not a particular policy stance, but rather a worldview that can be "activated" by leaders who are "willing to play on voters' fears and insecurities."[9]

A survey by Morning Consult meanwhile put the number of U.S. voters with right-wing authoritarian sentiments at 26 percent. Using a slightly different set of questions, it found a lower but still quite troubling percentage, and one that still poses significant risks for our political system. People exhibiting those traits were "more likely to reside in rural communities" and "more likely to report having no college degree."[10]

The two analyses agreed on one point, that playing to fear represents a primary mechanism that conservative leaders use to appeal to authoritarian voters. In a world of megachange where there are high levels of insecurity, it is easy to foster discontent and unhappiness. Many people have grievances, and it doesn't take much to appeal to those individuals. Technological change has disrupted entire industries, climate change is fueling extreme weather, income inequality has robbed millions of economic opportunity, and immigration and racial and ethnic diversity lead to intense fears about "the other" and concern regarding people who are different from oneself.[11]

It is a fertile environment for authoritarian leaders to encourage individuals to take the law into their own hands and overturn basic democratic principles. We saw this on January 6, 2021, when an angry mob incited by Trump stormed our nation's capitol and for a few hours delayed the certification of Biden's electoral victory. We see this in the rise of anti-Semitic attacks on Jews and violence directed at African Americans, Latinos, and Asian Americans. People's fears about the future safety and stability of the United States no longer appear overblown but rather reflect meaningful threats to our current situation.[12]

During the 2020 presidential election, for example, a number of Trump supporters expressed agreement with the viewpoint that "Trump should continue in office despite a loss if he declares [the] election was fixed and crooked." When asked about that, 19 percent of those who exhibited sympathy for social dominance favored Trump staying in office, and 23 percent of those who showed right-wing authoritarianism and support for social dominance thought he should remain in office due to allegations of election fraud.

Based on these results, researchers presciently concluded that "Trump does maintain a core base of high RWA/SDO (right-wing authoritarian and social dominance orientation) voters who might take to the ramparts for him."[13] The experts worried that significant numbers of Americans had the potential for violence and saw their opponents as engaging in unfair tactics.

A follow-up survey found a significant willingness among Trump voters to take undemocratic viewpoints and actions. Table 4-2 shows the breakdowns for right-wing authoritarian Trump voters, other Trump voters, and Biden voters, and the results are disturbing. Among highly authoritarian Trump voters, there was strong agreement that vote fraud changed the 2020 election outcome, that some GOP election officials who said there was no fraud were covering up evidence, that they would definitely support the installation of an alternate elector slate in states Biden narrowly won, and that they definitely believed the Trump campaign over judges who saw no evidence of voting irregularities.[14]

There were similar sentiments among other Trump voters, although not quite as pronounced as with his core base. Even those individuals who were not outright authoritarian in their viewpoints but still voted for him accepted problematic notions about the Deep State and election fraud. Nearly half of them said they were likely

TABLE 4-2. Beliefs of Right-Wing Authoritarian Trump Voters, Other Trump Voters, and Biden Voters, 2020

	Right-Wing Authoritarian Trump Voters (%)	Other Trump Voters (%)	Biden Voters (%)
Trump needed to bend rules in order to get things done	29	24	80
Deep State definitely trying to hurt Trump	93	62	0
Definitely agree that vote fraud changed 2020 election outcome	91	45	0
Strongly agree that Republican election officials who say there was no fraud are covering up evidence	62	27	0
Definitely support alternative elector slate in states Biden narrowly won	60	25	0
Definitely believe Trump campaign over judges who see no evidence of voting irregularities	56	41	0

Source: Patrick Murray, "Study Finds Differences between Two Types of Supporters," Monmouth University Polling Institute, January 19, 2021.

to believe the Trump campaign over judges on the subject of voting irregularities.

Virtually no Biden voter agreed with any of those premises, other than the one about Trump bending the rules in order to get things done. They believed the former chief executive had compromised many norms and laws, but did not accept allegations of vote fraud or unfair election practices. They did not mistrust judges and were not inclined to subvert democracy by installing alternative elector slates.

Yet other research has shown authoritarian sentiments among left-wing voters in the United States. Writer Sally Satel published an article in the *Atlantic* entitled "The Myth That Authoritarianism Happens Only on the Right." She cites research by Emory professor Thomas Costello documenting common features of conservative and liberal illiberalism, such as a "preference for social uniformity, prejudice towards different others, willingness to wield group authority to coerce behavior, cognitive rigidity, aggression and punitiveness towards perceived enemies, outsized concern for hierarchy, and moral absolutism." However, Costello estimates that "right-wing authoritarians outnumber left-wing ones by roughly three to one" in the United States, making the threat from the right more widespread than that from the left.[15]

Other national surveys have found concerning results about conservative illiberalism. For example, a 2018 Democracy Fund Voter Study Group survey analysis found that "Nearly a quarter of Americans say that a strong leader who doesn't have to bother with Congress or elections would be 'fairly' or 'very good.'"[16] Another poll by that organization undertaken after the 2020 election discovered that "46 percent of Republicans said that it would be appropriate for Republican state legislators to try to assign electoral votes to Trump in states won by Biden. Just 30 percent said it would be inappropriate [with about one-quarter unsure]."[17]

That stark repudiation of institutional checks and balances and democratic principles reveals the precarious state of American politics. Based on our deeply flawed information ecosystem, there is a wide gap among the public between the two parties, a loss of moderate political leadership, a lack of public trust, intolerance about the political opposition, and a willingness to consider undemocratic actions in order to alter electoral outcomes the person does not like.

When fueled by fake news, alternative facts, and false conspiracy theories, a social media environment filled with vitriol, a lack of respect for procedural justice, and a public that is cynical about everything related to politics, these viewpoints represent a classic formula for authoritarian government. Leaders can claim fraud, persuade their supporters of this grave injustice, appeal to the sense of grievance, and convince voters it is necessary to overturn the election results.

It is a playbook that has been seen in other nations, and the prevalence of these views among Trump supporters could lay the groundwork for future authoritarianism. The charges do not have to be true in order to serve as a rationale for mob action or overturning democratic elections. They just have to be credible enough that people are willing to take up arms on behalf of perceived injustices or that leaders are able to use public grievances to rig the system in favor of one party.

Since each of those things is already occurring in the United States, we need to take those risks very seriously going forward. These problems are no longer abstract threats; they are concrete mentalities being supported by significant portions of the general public. Leaders are playing to the false claims of election fraud and passing laws that restrict voting and place limits on political protest. They are stoking fears about political unfairness and inciting supporters to follow them down the road to authoritarianism.

5

Counter-Majoritarianism

Classic definitions of democracy emphasize the principles of popular will, majority rule, fair elections, equitable representation, and the protection of minority rights. The general ideas that distinguish democracy from monarchy, dictatorships, autocracy, illiberalism, and authoritarianism are the rule of law, procedural justice, fair representation in political institutions, and some correspondence between public opinion and public policy as long as the policy does not endanger basic rights.

Right now, American democracy is at risk on several fronts. It has laws that allow legal coups to take place, voting rights to be compromised, extremism that poisons civic discourse, a lack of public trust in government, and a toxic information ecosystem. This combination of features threatens basic elements of democratic self-rule.

But one of the little-appreciated contemporary challenges concerns the emergence of counter-majoritarianism that thwarts the popular will, distorts representation, and enables small groups of individuals to overrule the political majority, creating an unrepresentative system overall. The list of vehicles that enable these problems to flourish includes the following:

- The antiquated Electoral College

- A U.S. Senate that underrepresents large states and uses filibusters to let small groups of senators block majority action

- Gerrymandering in the national and state legislatures

- Federal court packing and unrepresentative courts

- Lax campaign finance rules that give political power to the few over the many

Harvard political scientists Steven Levitsky and Daniel Ziblatt describe these issues quite eloquently: "The Constitution's key counter-majoritarian features, such as the Electoral College and the U.S. Senate, have long been biased toward sparsely populated territories. But given that Democrats are increasingly the party of densely populated areas and Republicans dominate less populated areas, this long-standing rural bias now allows the Republican party to win the presidency, control Congress, and pack the Supreme Court *without winning electoral majorities.*"[1]

One little-known fact is that Republicans have won the presidential popular vote only once (in 2004 with the Bush-Kerry election) in the eight elections since 1992. Bill Clinton won the popular votes in 1992 and 1996, Albert Gore won it in 2000, Barack Obama scored the popular votes in 2008 and 2012, Hillary Clinton won it in 2016, and Joe Biden got it in 2020. But despite the lack of presidential popular vote success, the GOP has controlled the presidency in 12 of the 28 years between 1992 and 2020. Along with victories in U.S. Senate races and an unwillingness by senators to eliminate the filibuster, this institutional control has put them in a strong position to set the national agenda, dominate policymaking, and pack the Supreme Court and federal judiciary with conservative judges.[2]

Electoral College

One of the least democratic parts of the American political system is the Electoral College. Rather than direct popular election of the chief executive, the Founders created a body of "wise men" (women lacked the franchise) who would decide the presidency because of the suspicion large states would dominate the national government and a fear that uneducated mobs would seize control of public policymaking.[3]

According to Alexander Hamilton in *Federalist Paper* Number 68, the body was a compromise at the Constitutional Convention between large and small states. Many of the latter worried that states such as Massachusetts, New York, Pennsylvania, and Virginia would control the presidency so they devised an institution where each state had Electoral College votes in proportion to the number of its senators and House members. The former advantaged small states since each state had two senators regardless of its size.

But delegates also had an antimajoritarian concern in mind. At a time when many people were not well educated, they wanted a body that would deliberate over leading contenders and choose the best man for the presidency. They explicitly rejected a popular vote for president because they did not trust voters to make wise choices. The Founders wanted a buffer between popular rule and government decisionmaking so that leader choices would protect the country from unreasonable public sentiments. It was a fateful choice that now under certain circumstances could open the door to autocracy and undemocratic rule through perfectly lawful means.

The problem right now is that at a time of high income inequality and substantial geographic disparities across states, the Electoral College systematically overrepresents small areas that are not very prosperous over larger ones that are doing well economically. That combination poses serious problems for the political system as currently constituted.

That structure is problematic at a time when a Brookings Metropolitan Policy program study found that about 15 percent of American counties generate 70 percent of America's gross domestic product.[4] Most of the country's economic activity is on the East Coast, West Coast, and a few metropolitan areas in between. The prosperous parts of America now include around fifteen states having thirty senators, whereas the less prosperous areas encapsulate thirty-five states having seventy senators.

Those numbers demonstrate the highly challenging mismatch between population size, economic vitality, and political power. Through the Electoral College, the thirty-five states with lower economic activity have disproportionate power to choose presidents and dictate public policy. This institutional relic enables discrepancies between the popular and Electoral College votes as occurred in 2000 and 2016. Rather than being a historic aberration, candidates who lose the popular vote but become president emblemize an anti-majoritarian development where small numbers of voters in a handful of states can use their institutional clout to control the country's top position, override public opinion in the rest of the country, and block legislation desired by large numbers of people. It is a ticking time bomb that could explode our political system.

U.S. Senate

The U.S. Senate is another body that impedes democratic representation. The Constitution grants two senators to every state regardless of population size. This means that Wyoming, with 578,000 residents, has the same representation as California, with nearly 40 million residents, a clearly inequitable outcome. In conjunction with the economic activity numbers noted earlier, the result is that economically stagnant areas end up electing two-thirds of U.S. senators while the prosperous states control only one-third.

This is a formula for political disaster. Having that wide of a disparity between political and economic forces leads to a system with severe problems in terms of fairness and representation. It fuels political resentment of the sort that catapulted Donald Trump into the presidency and pits region against region in unhealthy ways. Since the Senate approves federal judges and controls international treaties, its lack of representativeness is particularly important to the manner in which the national government operates.

As a sign of how undemocratic the Senate has become, consider the results of the 2018 election. In that year, Senate Democrats outpolled Republicans by 18 million votes yet they lost two seats overall. And in 2022, analysts estimate that if Senate Democrats win by 4 percentage points nationally, they would only have a "50-50 chance of holding the majority." There is not an even match between votes and seats in the Senate because the body overrepresents small states and therefore distorts political control.[5]

Over the coming years, as the technology revolution unfolds and generates considerable economic inequality, the ingredients are in place for even greater representation problems. There could be a full-blown political backlash from voters who are angry that their geographic areas are stagnating and not sharing in the prosperity of the two coasts. Because of the institutional framework of U.S. governance, they will be in a strong position to express their anger and block what they believe are ill-advised actions. Unless the discontent associated with serious economic disparities is addressed, public unhappiness and an unrepresentative institution could stymie needed policy responses and exacerbate existing social and economic tensions in the United States.

In addition, the institutional dysfunction is furthered by internal rules that allow small numbers of members to stop action desired by the majority of senators. The option of a filibuster (or unlimited debate) that requires 60 of 100 members to stop the discussion effectively gives 41 senators the power to block action even where there is strong majority support. As a sign of the increasing frequency with which this tactic is being used, a Brennan Center for Justice analysis found that "There have been as many cloture motions [to end filibusters] in the last 10 years (959) . . . as there were during the 60-year period from 1947 to 2006 (960)."[6] The filibuster and other rules compound the lack of fairness in the Senate and contribute to the crisis of contemporary American democracy.

Gerrymandering

Gerrymandering is a practice by which legislators draw district lines in ways that provide major advantages to the party in power. Named after Elbridge Gerry, a nineteenth-century Massachusetts legislator and vice president in the James Madison administration who pioneered the practice, it has become widely used as a way to cement party control of the U.S. House of Representatives and in state legislatures.

Ideally, in a democratic system, you want a legislature with a seat–vote ratio of 1.0. That means if a party wins 52 percent of the vote, it gets 52 percent of the legislative seats—a 1 to 1 representation. A ratio at that level means there is a high degree of fairness and equity in the political system and representation where the institutional composition matches electoral sentiments.

Yet the U.S. House and many state legislatures are far from that kind of egalitarianism because they yield a higher percentage of seats than warranted based on the vote totals. For example, in Wisconsin in recent years, Republicans have held a favorable seat–vote ratio because they gerrymandered state legislative districts in their own favor. Wisconsin Democrats must win by several percentage points in the popular vote to achieve a bare majority of seats in the state legislature.[7]

This is not an unusual situation. In an analysis by Kyle Kondik of the University of Virginia, a number of states draw district lines in ways that favor the party in power. That leads to unrepresentative legislatures and unfair advantages for the ruling party. For example, he cites the case of Pennsylvania, which, with party control of the legislature after 2010, used its clout to generate a "lopsided 13-5 Republican edge in an otherwise competitive state."[8] He shows how Democrats did the same thing in Michigan and picked up two more seats out of fourteen that they would otherwise have gained based on the popular vote.

These types of political shenanigans skew American democracy and allow small groups of voters to block or overturn majority sentiments. It leads to unfair institutions, rigged elections, and public cynicism about how the process operates. Left unchecked, it corrodes democratic values and pushes the system in unfair and inequitable directions.

Federal Court-Packing

The courts are designed to uphold the rule of law and protect fundamental rights. As the third branch of the national government, they are crucial to procedural justice and the protection of individual rights. Justices and judges rule on major cases, and as the unelected branch, they are supposed to rise above politics and represent fundamental legal principles.

Yet, in recent years, federal courts have been tilted in a conservative direction. The Supreme Court has a 6–3 conservative majority after Leader Mitch McConnell refused to act on President Obama's nomination of Merrick Garland to fill the seat of the late Antonin Scalia. McConnell's refusal to act took a seat that would have been filled by a Democratic president and turned it into a conservative seat now held by Justice Neil Gorsuch. And when liberal Justice Ruth Ginsberg passed away during the Trump presidency, Republicans filled that seat with conservative jurist Amy Coney Barrett. Similar actions have occurred at the federal judge level, with Republicans adding a number of conservative jurists to the federal courts.

This raises important questions regarding the ability of judges to rise above political pressures and the impartiality of justice. In countries such as Poland and Hungary, which have moved in an illiberal direction, the ruling party has packed the courts with like-minded judges and undermined the rule of law. Rather than serve as a check and balance on elected officials, many of the new judges vote in line with the ruling party and subvert the fairness of the legal process.

The growing unrepresentativeness of federal courts is problematic because it leads to the perception and possible reality of unfairness, political bias, and injustice. The politicization of the judiciary is a hallmark of illiberal democracies and authoritarian governments, and Americans need to keep a close eye on that branch in order to ensure that our nation does not move further down that path.

Lax Campaign Finance Rules

Money in politics and campaign finance represents the starkest example of the power of the few over the many. Those who contribute represent a small percentage of overall Americans and tilt the system in favor of those with large financial resources. Contributors are not typical in their viewpoints, and they move public policy in unrepresentative ways. With income inequality at a 100-year high in the United States, the disparity in the ability to give introduces serious inequity into the political process.[9]

The wealthy are much more politically active than the general public. In a survey of "economically successful Americans," political scientists Benjamin Page, Larry Bartels, and Jason Seawright measured the activism and beliefs of the ultrarich.[10] In questioning these individuals, the researchers found that 99 percent of the wealthy said they voted in presidential elections, far higher than the rate of the general public. Two-thirds (68 percent) made campaign contributions to politicians, which is far higher than the 14 percent of the general public that contributes.

More problematic from the standpoint of systemic fairness,

though, is the fact that the superrich hold policy views that are significantly more conservative than ordinary citizens. In their survey, Page, Bartels, and Seawright asked the wealthy about a range of public policy issues and found that top wealth holders "differ rather sharply from the American public on a number of important policies. For example, there are significant differences on issues such as taxation, economic regulation, and social welfare programs."[11] The wealthy are more likely than the general public to favor cuts in Medicare and education (58 percent versus 27 percent for the public), while they are less likely than the public to believe that the government has an essential role in regulating the market (55 percent versus 71 percent, respectively).

Those with tremendous financial resources are far more conservative than the public on issues related to social opportunity, education, and health care. They do not support a major role for the public sector, even when government actions further economic and social opportunities for the general public. They are much more likely to favor cuts in social benefits and programs that benefit less fortunate members of society. These views of the superrich led them to favor tax cuts and place more emphasis on deficit reduction than on "pump-priming" that stimulates broad-based economic growth. If politically active rich people favor tax cuts and oppose opportunity measures, as has been the case in recent years, it is difficult to generate political support for programs that help the nation's low- and middle-income people better themselves.

Unrepresentative System

Taken together, the emergence of so many counter-majoritarian institutions and processes in the United States during the contemporary period poses grave risks for the overall system. It undermines the popular will, fails to serve majority interests, is neither fair nor impartial, and allows small groups of voters to undermine basic democratic values. In a number of cases, our current regime has features that enable the few consistently to triumph over the many, which furthers public cynicism about government and turns political contests into unfettered power politics.

As a sign of how far America has sunk, an overtime analysis undertaken by the Freedom House organization found that the United States had dropped eleven points on a democracy scale from a decade ago. Due to problems such as gerrymandering, voting restrictions, large and secret money in politics, and racial injustice, the country had a democracy that ranked below nations such as Argentina and Mongolia and similar to flawed systems such as those in Romania and Panama.[12]

During a highly polarized time period where opponents dislike one another, there is a serious risk of a constitutional crisis that will be resolved with a legal coup or through undemocratic means. As noted at the beginning of this volume, the Electoral Count Act of 1887 and the Insurrection Act of 1807 allow a legal coup in which states can contest an election, overturn the popular vote, send the unrepresentative slate of electors to Congress, and have that body certify Electoral College votes that allow the losing candidate to win the presidency.

Such an outcome would send the country into turmoil and create the possibility of large-scale public protests that would destabilize the nation. With the ability to declare emergency powers and call out state and federal troops to restore order, a president could engineer a de facto coup and then use its power in government to rig future elections. Although such a result might seem far-fetched, the basis exists for that type of situation, and it is quite conceivable given a tribal political culture, a toxic information system, institutional unfairness, voter suppression, and a lack of respect for procedural justice. It may be the case that a country that is already in chaos has the foundation for even greater illiberalism.

6

Knowledge Threats

During normal times, issues of endangerment do not loom very large. The risks are manageable, and there aren't many surprises that can upend your life. There is less chaos and more predictability in terms of how things happen. People don't go to work each day wondering whether the system is at risk, what is going to go wrong, who is going to ambush them, or who will blame them for bad things that take place.

But these are not "normal" times. Facts are in dispute, and it is a highly partisan environment. Powerful people can create major trouble for you; they can besmirch organizations, investigate people, and generate negative press. It poisons the well for all who seek to undertake thoughtful analysis of contemporary issues.

For many parts of the knowledge sector, Trump and his supporters pose discernible threats to democratic discourse and operations. In their book *Unmaking the Presidency*, Susan Hennessey and Ben Wittes chronicle the misdeeds, dashed norms, abusive practices, and outright deceits that characterized the former president's time in government.[1] He treated the attorney general as his personal legal representative and asked government officials, law enforcement agents, foreign leaders, and diplomats to aid his campaign and investigate his political opponents.[2]

Yet Trumpistas are not the only threats. There are a variety of ways in which wealthy individuals, sensationalized reporting, ideologues of all stripes, and geopolitical developments have disrupted knowledge creation and dissemination. Universities, think tanks, and nonprofit organizations face a number of challenges to their academic freedom and research independence. These are important dangers because democracy requires a vibrant civil society in order to promote healthy dialogue, discourse, and deliberation.

The Ultrawealthy

Over the last decade, think tanks and universities have gone through many trials and tribulations associated with Trump and his allies in government, business, and the news media. During his time in office, the chief executive recast politics in ways that disturbed those in many organizations, including experts in the right of center space. A number of conservative academics worried about Trump's antidemocratic tendencies and lack of respect for procedural justice.

In a startling first-person account entitled "Think Tank in the Tank," former Manhattan Institute senior fellow Sol Stern (also a contributing editor to the Manhattan Institute's *City Journal*) alleged overt censorship and staff terminations at his organization as a result of critical writing about Trump. Even though many of its scholars warned about Trump's dangers to democracy and civil discourse, Stern claimed that some of its trustees and leading donors pressured the Institute's leaders to move the think tank in a direction that was supportive of President Trump.[3]

According to Stern, critical articles got quashed, and pieces supportive of the president were favored. Two years into Trump's presidency, Stern resigned "to protest the magazine's intellectual abdication on the most urgent crisis facing the nation today; the election of an unfit, dangerous man to the presidency." He described some of its trustees as "accomplice[s] in one of the most malignant political movements in the country."[4] For him, it was a sign of wealthy donors endangering academic freedom and creating challenges for the knowledge sector.

But concern over trustee interference is not limited to the conservative-oriented Manhattan Institute. There have been allegations from other think tanks of board members engaging in intrusive behaviors. Wealthy businesspeople are protective of their low tax rates and not shy about criticizing experts whose work suggested that high earners should pay more in taxes and whose businesses should be subject to greater government oversight.[5] Also, a number of trustees do not like the work of scholars in various places who call U.S. society racist and argue in favor of reparations to redress centuries of racial injustice.

Similar problems emerged at leading universities as wealthy donors object to curricular designs and programmatic choices they do not like. At Yale University, for example, Beverly Gage, the director of the Brady-Johnson Program in Grand Strategy, resigned, saying "the university failed to stand up for academic freedom amid inappropriate efforts by its donors to influence its curriculum and faculty hiring."[6] After one of the program's professors wrote an opinion piece entitled, "How to Protect America from the Next Donald Trump," donor Nicholas Brady complained to university officials about the article and said "this is not what Charles Johnson and I signed up for." In response to this complaint, Yale set up a new advisory board composed mainly of conservative Republicans, including former secretary of state Henry Kissinger, and Brady indicated he wanted someone to observe program courses and report back on what was being taught. At that point, Gage asked the university to protect her academic freedom and later resigned over what she felt was an inadequate response from the institution. "It's very difficult to teach effectively or creatively in a situation where you are being second-guessed and undermined and not protected," she said.[7]

That case was illustrative of the many ways in which wealth is corrupting both politics and civil society. In her book, *Dark Money*, writer Jane Mayer outlines the billionaires who are subverting "think tanks, academic institutions, media groups, courthouses, and government allies" through their immense financial resources. She sees them as a threat to democracy because of their "carefully concealed agendas steering the nation." In particular, Mayer worried about conservative billionaires who funded the radical right due to the amount of money they spent and the self-interested agenda they pursued.[8]

The Trump era was not the first time people were concerned about the influence of the ultrarich. In a 2014 book entitled *Billionaires*, I had bemoaned the "wealthification" of America in which rich interests were taking over publicly minded organizations and pushing them toward corporate viewpoints. Income inequality had grown in recent decades to a century-long high, and there were extremes of both wealth and poverty in America.[9]

Tufts University professor Dan Drezner has warned in his book, *The Ideas Industry*, that high levels of wealth concentration are risky for the knowledge sector. He talks about how plutocrats are transforming the "marketplace of ideas" and skewing ideation in partisan directions.[10] We have seen evidence of that trend in the rise of neoliberal economics, the triumph of the market over government regulation, the gutting of campaign finance laws, the rise of dark money, and the emphasis on the financial and political virtues of globalization.

I had been attuned to the power of the wealthy long before I had interviewed for my job at Brookings. For a number of decades, Brown University had been a school of the children of the rich and famous. There were sons and daughters of prominent political and media figures. And wealthy families from all around the world sent their children to be educated at the Ivy League university.[11]

During my 2008 interview with Brookings president Strobe Talbott, I had jokingly told him that "fundraising is the only part of my life where I am a socialist." Rich people had a lot of money during a time of high income inequality, and our job was to get some of it back so we could use it for positive philanthropic purposes. There had been a long pause as that remark sank in, and he finally responded, "That is a good line, but don't use it in front of our trustees."

I got the job despite my brash comment, but years later, the mere possibility of my *Billionaires* book highlighting the problems of ultrawealth had created considerable tension at the highest level of the institution. Talbott was unhappy I had written a book about wealthy interests, and in an unusual move required his personal review and approval before the book was published. To his credit, though, he let the book go forward on academic freedom grounds. But he was not pleased that I had written on a topic that might upset our donors even though inequality was clearly central to America's political dysfunction.

High-Stakes Conflict

When I was growing up, the classic advice in my rural hometown was "don't get into a pissing match with a skunk." The reason was obvious as it was clear you wouldn't come out of that encounter smelling very good. Skunks have a way of polluting the scene with odors that will linger for a long time.

The same adage applies to politics—encounters with the occasional human skunk leave a foul aroma all around. Those kinds of individuals fight dirty, engage in unscrupulous activities, weaponize information, and challenge the integrity of everyone else. After all, if they can make supporters believe that everyone is corrupt, then corruption drops out as a factor in penalizing those who are truly unethical.

In Rhode Island, where I had spent most of my adult life, one common tactic for attacking the opposition was "dropping a dime" in a pay phone. This was before the time of mobile phones and surveillance cameras, when one could place an anonymous call and report negative information on your enemies. It was a time-worn technique used in political campaigns as well as in efforts to take down opponents. Without revealing your personal identity, you simply called a reporter or law enforcement agent and pointed that person in the direction of your adversary. It was quick, effective, and anonymous.

In D.C., this tactic has been displaced by the "art of the leak." Confidential calls to friendly reporters or government investigators who promise never to reveal the source are the way to ensure positive action and facilitate critical stories about others. It represents a technique to spin the news with the help of sympathetic reporters. People feed journalists negative stories, and the journalists get exclusive stories in return. It works out great, except for the object of the leak, who becomes the subject of a scathing news article.

In the contemporary period, where the public is highly suspicious of anything associated with the capitol city, there are many ways to weaken opponents. You can investigate them, challenge their credibility, or, in the case of nonprofits, pull their tax-exempt status, which will eliminate the deductibility of charitable contributions to the organization. The latter, of course, is the nuclear option against think tanks, universities, and nonprofits.

Even though impeachment represented a profound action, a number of my academic colleagues plus many Americans felt the grounds for Trump's removal were quite valid. They felt he had abused the powers of his office with respect to the president of Ukraine by suggesting that he would withhold congressionally approved assistance unless the foreign leader announced an investigation of Trump's leading Democratic opponent. When reproached for these activities, he threatened opponents, filed lawsuits, and undermined basic norms of the political system. Ultimately, Trump's stance was that he had not broken any law.

For our organization, the contentiousness surrounding Trump

came to a head with the unmasking of the whistleblower whose memo about the Ukrainian phone call had sparked the initial investigation. This was the key action that had brought Trump's actions to light and spurred the House impeachment.

After his damaging call to Ukraine's president Volodymyr Zelensky was revealed, Trump supporters pointed to a Central Intelligence Agency analyst as the likely source of the leak. Almost immediately, the conservative *Breitbart* website published a story linking that individual by name to Hillary Clinton, Barack Obama, Joe Biden, and the Brookings Institution.[12] The article noted that the whistleblower had worked in the White House for Tori Nuland, who was a confidant of then president Strobe Talbott and held a nonresident senior fellow position at our institution. The implication was that the investigation was purely political, and there was a Democratic conspiracy to take down the chief executive.

Within a few hours, a Twitter post promoting the story was liked 100,000 times. Soon conservatives were peddling the story that Ukraine, not Russia, had interfered in the 2016 election in order to help Democrats. The narrative was a follow-up to earlier right-wing claims that Obama was a closet Muslim and Hillary Clinton a secret pedophile. The false charge turned the Trump impeachment on its head and claimed that Democrats were the ones committing a gross injustice, not the GOP president.

It wasn't long before President Trump retweeted a post revealing the actual name of the alleged whistleblower, in apparent violation of federal rules against whistleblower identification and retaliation. That tweet led former Bush speechwriter David Frum to label Trump a "gangster" president who was breaking the law.[13]

Conservatives publicized a narrative that my colleague Ben Wittes, who ran a popular blog called *Lawfare*, was knee-deep in the conspiracy because a few years earlier he had argued that Democrats needed an "insurance policy" in case Trump won the 2016 election. According to conservative skeptics, that policy involved all-out attacks on Trump and eventually impeachment itself.

Writer Sharyl Attkisson was a proponent of that argument, saying, "We continue to get evidence of an orchestrated effort among government insiders and the well-connected to take down President Trump at all costs."[14]

As conservative fears about this alleged "conspiracy" spread, right-wing outlets openly attacked the Brookings Institution. For example, Julie Kelly of the far-right Center for American Greatness argued Brookings was a "laundering agent of sorts for Democratic political contributions," and its scholars were engaging in "one of the biggest frauds in history on the American people."[15] In another piece, she complained that my colleagues were writing "collusion propaganda articles disguised as think pieces."[16]

In a similar light, Joe Hoft of the ultra-right Gateway Pundit website summarized the critique of Brookings with the following headline: "With Huge Financial Backing from Hostile Foreign Entities Brookings Institute Is Working to Help Democrats Win in 2020." He argued that Brookings should be shut down for violating its nonprofit, tax-exempt status by engaging in partisan lobbying and overt campaigning.[17]

Neither of these sites had much credibility with the political mainstream, but they had an important ally in Donald Trump. He loved these and other websites precisely because they published stories with sensationalistic headlines. White House officials said they regularly found the chief executive waving stories from the Gateway Pundit and other right-wing sites and berating his staff for not "following the internet the way I do."[18] They should pay attention to the coverage, he argued, because those outlets understood the really nefarious stuff taking place in American politics. He would retweet their far-fetched stories and then watch conservative politicians and television outlets follow his lead on television.

Congressman Devin Nunes poured gasoline on the conspiracy story in 2020 when he went on Fox News with Maria Bartiromo and said the Brookings Institution through its former president Strobe Talbott had disseminated the infamous anti-Trump dossier compiled by Christopher Steele, a former British intelligence officer. That document had included a number of highly inflammatory charges against Trump that had infuriated the presidential candidate. Speaking of Brookings employees, Nunes claimed on the prominent national television show that "they were involved for sure in the dissemination and for sure in the defense of the dossier."[19]

Other outlets added fuel to the inferno. RealClearInvestigations reported that Igor "Iggy" Danchenko, a former Brookings research assistant in 2010 for Fiona Hill, had served as one of the chief compilers of the Steele dossier. According to the article, Steele had hired Danchenko to "dig up dirt on Trump and Russia for the Hillary Clinton campaign," and that information laid the groundwork for the 2016 FBI investigation into Trump."[20]

Conservatives had a field day with the disclosures. Reporters wrote stories complaining about the "far-left-leaning Brookings Institution" while congressional staffers threatened Brookings's legal status, saying in stories and opinion pieces that "their 501(c)(3) status should be audited, because they are a major player in the dossier deal."[21]

People's fears inside Brookings intensified when after these stories appeared, one of our colleagues was targeted in a U.S. Department of Homeland Security (DHS) intelligence gathering effort. That agency's handling of political protests in Portland, Oregon, and the sending of unidentified federal agents to that city had come under fire, and Wittes and a *New York Times* reporter had published information from unclassified DHS memos. Among the documents was one conceding that "camouflaged federal agents sent to put down the unrest in Portland didn't understand the nature of the protests they were facing."[22]

Upset with the media leaks, DHS officials in its Office of Intelligence and Analysis compiled "intelligence reports" on Wittes and *Times* reporter Mike Baker. Generally used for terrorists and violent criminals, these reports are sent to law enforcement agents to aid their work. Former administration officials reacted strongly to the administration's tactics and argued that these reports should not be used against journalists and academics. That action was "bizarre," according to former DHS General Counsel Steve Bunnell, and "has nothing to do with DHS's original mission."[23]

Some observers worried that this surreptitious step represented a move in the direction of illegal oversight and could become a precursor to compiling dossiers on administration critics. The ordeal contributed to scholars' fears that retaliatory measures could escalate against Brookings on the part of Trump's supporters in Congress and federal agencies.

The risk in this kind of situation was not so much losing a legal action as incurring huge fees that would be very costly to those involved. For example, Ambassador Gordon Sondland incurred $1.8 million in legal fees during Trump's impeachment trial. His situation was expensive because he had to testify before Congress, reconstruct detailed itineraries and conversations, get legal advice regarding the complicated issues involved in that case, and not incriminate himself during hours of testimony.[24]

On the last day of 2020, the Trump administration threw a fastball at Brookings by subpoenaing the personnel records of Igor Danchenko, the individual who undertook research for the Steele dossier. Special Counsel John Dunham demanded documents relating to Danchenko's employment, even though it had been a decade since he had worked at Brookings, and press reports indicated that there was nothing in his file that related to the dossier.[25]

After an investigation, Danchenko was arrested in 2021 on charges of lying to federal investigators.[26] Within days of that indictment, the meme #ArrestFionaHill was trending on Twitter and being shared thousands of times in what appeared to be a highly coordinated manner. This was accompanied by critical stories claiming that "Brookings was ground zero for the Russia collusion hoax, with many key staff embroiled in the damaging lie that Donald Trump colluded with Vladimir Putin to steal the 2016 election."[27] Fox News published an article on its website by George Washington University law professor Jonathan Turley entitled "This Liberal Think Tank Keeps Popping Up in Durham Investigation."[28]

These activities represented just some of the ways others sought to pin blame on critics for the years-long investigations into the suspicious ties between Trump and Russia, and Trump's efforts to dig up dirt on Joe Biden with foreign leaders. Rather than deal substantively with the charge that Trump had abused his office, both the president and his political supporters played a blame game that rejected the investigations as overly partisan and a sign of unfair behavior on the part of opponents.

A number of individuals used all possible means to tarnish the opposition and bring the public to their side. They filed legal motions, used partisan media sites to smear critics, and condemned the opposition through social media attacks. Several people sent death threats to Brookings experts in order to make sure that the experts understood the depth of their anger.

Twenty-five percent of our Governance Studies residential scholars received death threats, which to me, represented a shockingly high number. One graphic phone call warned, "I am going to wipe the entire Brookings Institution off the face of the fucking earth. You are scum sucking evil motherfuckers and you all deserve death in the most heinous way and it's coming at you."[29]

In dealing with this subject, I learned about gradations of death threats from the more general to the more specific. A general death threat takes the form of "you should be killed" without listing the particular time or place, and with the threat taking the form of a "passive voice." Among this genre, it is generally seen as the least worrisome concerning the intent to inflict harm. But there are more explicit formulations, such as, "I am going to kill you" to "you live on X Street and I am going to kill you" to "I know you have a spouse named X and children named Y and Z, and I am going to kill you."

When I moved to D.C. more than a decade ago, I never thought I would have to deal with these kinds of abusive threats and security risks.

Mercurial Senators

During my time in the capitol city, I also learned to be very careful in dealing with mainstream senators. Being a member of one of the most exclusive clubs in the country and having the ability to hold up appointments and stop legislation through a filibuster made them (along with the president and Supreme Court Justices) the most powerful people in town. Everyone was completely deferential to them, realizing the tremendous power each held and the fact that individual senators had the ability to give or withhold major public benefits in the form of tax provisions, federal appointments, or broad policy actions.

One day, we were fortunate to get a senator for one of our events. At the appointed time, the particular individual showed up, and we ushered him into a small room. He immediately lit into his staff. What was this bill about, he inquired? When told of its major provisions, he interrupted by asking, "Why are we supporting the bill?" Some of the legislative sections apparently contained policies that he actually opposed. His young staff was left to explain that one of the Senate cosponsors had insisted on certain provisions as a condition for supporting the legislation.

The senator was incredibly grouchy and not ashamed of his bad mood. "It is a garbage bill," he told his staff, and he didn't understand provisions that were in it. When one of his staffers slowly attempted to explain a main point, the senator countered by saying, "Pick it up. I have been to law school and don't have all day with the explanation."

Turning to me, he asked who was doing his introduction? Realizing the minefield into which I was stepping, I hesitantly told him I was introducing him and gave him a short sense of what I planned to say. "You only have three of my committees," he warned, and the introduction omitted key parts of his background. Pivoting to his press secretary, he reprimanded her by saying, "You should have sent him better information." I felt badly because it wasn't her fault; I had prepared my introduction based on material from his website and edited it down because he was someone who was well known and did not need a lengthy description.

Attempting to defuse what was quickly becoming a deteriorating conversation, I asked him what he wanted me to say in the event introduction. That turned out to be the magic gesture as the senator noted that he had led major organizations and served on many important committees. I dutifully took notes and incorporated his comments in my introduction, which pleased him enormously.

As soon as we were on stage, the senator's dour mood evaporated, and he was friendly, funny, and incredibly well informed on the legislation that he had just privately told us he didn't understand and didn't like. Without missing a beat, he incorporated advice one of my colleagues had given him about the proposal and came across as smart and knowledgeable. After the event, he was all smiles. He loved how the forum went, was incredibly friendly, and stayed to talk for a considerable time.

Despite his initial furor, he thanked me for organizing a great forum. I was stunned by the abrupt turnaround, but glad things had moved in my favor. Yet I remained surprised at how quickly the mood could shift with this powerful man, and the whole experience reminded me how tumultuous D.C. politics could be, even with leaders who were well respected and considered to be highly responsible. There were few constraints on the whims of influential senators, and I saw firsthand how their individual predilections could shift very quickly.

Hardball Tactics

Think tanks are not immune to hardball tactics, both within and between organizations. Although the atmosphere is typically genial, there are some individuals who weaponize information through email blind carbon copies (bccs) or the forwarding of messages. Anything you put in writing in digital form could be used by others to advance their own causes. One person loved to engage in palace intrigue via bccs. The only problem was that in a relatively small organization, others became aware of this proclivity and were careful what they sent.

Others were more upfront about their sharp elbows. When I first arrived at Brookings in 2008, I was about to publish a Brookings book entitled *Digital Health*, which dealt with health information technology. Because we had common interests, I expected the director of the Brookings health care center to be interested in my research. I requested a "get to know you" meeting, and for months got no response. Eventually, his deputy met with me and told me in no uncertain terms that I should not be working on health care because that was their issue and no one outside their center could work on that topic. In case I didn't take his admonition seriously, he followed our conversation with a complaint to the president, warning I should stay away from health care research.

To our then head Strobe Talbott's credit, that stunning request was not approved. He followed a "no lanes" policy at Brookings and said as long as you had appropriate expertise, you could write on various areas of interest. The encounter was a sobering reminder, however, that I needed to be careful of those within the organization who had particular interests and be mindful of their ability to create trouble for me.

Challenging circumstances were apparent in other D.C.-based think tanks as well. The conservative-leaning American Enterprise Institute (AEI) went through a "near-death" experience in the mid-1980s due to poor financial management.[30] It faced an aggressive competitor in the form of the Heritage Foundation, which put a vast amount of money into political advocacy and cultivated close relations on Capitol Hill and in federal agencies. AEI was forced to make a number of hard choices, but came out of that period as a strong and well-respected research entity.

I had my own dustup with someone from Heritage. After I published a Brookings piece on ways to encourage the news media to move toward more thoughtful and less polarized discourse, I was attacked by one of its people. In an article, a Heritage writer complained that I wanted "a centralized state composed of luminaries making enlightened decisions for the rest of society." While he publicly conceded that I was not authoritarian or totalitarian, he said I wanted to "ban actions, speech or even thought deemed 'hateful,' 'anti-social,' 'against social conviviality,' and so on."[31] Most surprising, though, was that right after his article appeared, he called me up and wanted to go to lunch to show me he actually was a nice guy. I passed on that invitation, steaming over his misrepresentation of my views.

The Aspen Institute was another organization that encountered rough winds in 2020 during the major economic downturn associated with the coronavirus pandemic. Many people across the country became ill, and a number of organizations fell on hard times. The economy collapsed when employers sent their people home and consumer spending dropped precipitously. In short order, unemployment rose to double-digit levels, and there were eerie comparisons to the Great Depression of the 1930s.

Aspen raised much of its money by doing events, holding high-profile conferences, and attracting prominent individuals to its various campuses around the world. Its exclusive invitations propelled the organization to great heights as a place where "movers and shakers" congregated and rubbed elbows with the rich and famous. With the downturn, however, that business model collapsed. No longer able to hold in-person events or sponsor conferences, its revenues fell, and the organization projected losses of $14 to $17 million, which was more than 10 percent of its annual operating revenue.[32]

Around this time, Congress enacted the Paycheck Protection Program bill designed to provide relief to hard-hit organizations. It was a way to keep organizations solvent while the economy recovered. Aspen applied for and was granted $8 million in federal assistance by the Small Business Administration. It planned to use the money to save jobs and sustain the organization.

But one of its experts objected to the relief and publicly criticized his own institution in the press. He argued, "The people and businesses—local bookstores, coffee shops, restaurants, small foundries, little packaging businesses, your local grocers—that really need the money have none. We have Depression-era unemployment. Mass deaths. And one of America's most elite institutions thinks it is okay to take the money. Those who purport to be values-based and public-spirited leaders cannot at the same time put self-interest first, when there is so much human suffering and death."[33]

An Aspen spokesperson defended the decision to seek the money. Amy DeMaria explained, "We applied for PPP funds because we have suffered a serious hit to our budget, and are doing everything possible to keep our people employed—which is the purpose of the PPP program." Its leaders were clearly worried about the institution's financial viability since it was not clear how long the downturn would last and when Aspen would resume its high-profile events and conferences.

Within a day of the critical news article, however, Aspen announced it was returning the money. In a statement, DeMaria explained "We believe that our application, which was made in the first week of the PPP, was consistent with the goals of the program. Upon listening to our communities and further reflection, we have made the decision to return the loan. The Aspen Institute is committed to doing our part to help the country and the world both recover from and rebuild after this global pandemic. We stand with all who are trying to make a difference in very difficult times."[34]

There also were disputes within the Atlantic Council. After two experts argued that "the U.S. should not focus on human rights in its dealings with Russia," two dozen of their own colleagues signed a public letter disagreeing with that stance and attributing the soft position on Russia to funding received from a conservative foundation. One of the signers anonymously complained to a reporter, saying, "The reputational risk . . . [is] that we're willing to give our good name to arguments that amount to we ought to give Putin a free hand at home including to murder political opponents, and invade his neighbors when he really feels he needs to."[35]

On an artificial intelligence book published by Brookings, I faced challenges within my own institution. Some did not want the book to come out and pushed for reviewers who would say it was unpublishable. Fortunately for me, that effort did not work because the peer reviewers liked the book and recommended it for publication. The book went on to a warm reception, and six months later, Brookings' AI policy work was rated number one in the world by the University of Pennsylvania.[36]

Waving the Money Flag

Fundraising is a political vulnerability for every nonprofit organization because each entity has to raise money in order to operate. Although Brookings had a sizeable endowment of $450 million, which funded a significant portion of our activities, and we had donors of varying perspectives and backgrounds, most think tanks did not have those kinds of reserves and were dependent on a limited number of donors.

In a highly polarized environment with a heavy emphasis on political combat and when money is a contentious issue, fundraising often becomes the vehicle by which people criticize think tanks, universities, and news organizations. Just as political candidates long ago learned it was easier to attack the opposition's source of funding than the competitor's substantive ideas, the same vulnerability became apparent in the knowledge sector. It was easy to jump from the fact that someone is providing money to the idea that institutes are completely corrupt because of outside funding. Waving the money flag became a common tactic for those who wanted to challenge expertise and go after specific organizations.

There would be all-out campaigns to attack newspapers, universities, and think tanks based on their financing. For example, former president Trump loved to complain about what he called the "Amazon *Washington Post*," a not very subtle reference to the fact that the paper was owned by billionaire Jeff Bezos. Trump was unhappy with the paper's frequent fact-checking and wanted people to see it as a corporate tool of the wealthy businessman. Its reporters asked tough questions of him, identified abuses at his businesses and foundations, and documented tens of thousands of falsehoods during his years in office.[37]

In a world where the public was extremely cynical about money in politics, and funding was a vulnerability, adversaries knew they could raise doubts about any organization simply by alleging malfeasance due to funding sources. It didn't matter where the money came from or whether there was evidence of unethical behavior. A skeptical public would believe if your newspaper was owned by a billionaire, or if a nonprofit took money from a specific entity, you were beholden to that individual or organization. You could have a big endowment, hundreds of donors, disclose the contributors, receive financing from people with conflicting points of view, and engage in independent scholarly work, but still look guilty in the court of public opinion.

In an era of widespread cynicism, opponents would weaponize financial information in dangerous ways and use funding controversies to discredit authoritative institutional gatekeepers. Anything that undermined fact-checkers or outside experts was advantageous for those who wanted to weaken democracy. They knew that if they could challenge academic expertise and delegitimize university scholarship, it would be easy to troll opponents, inflame the public, and spread false information regarding vaccines, climate change, and ballot fraud.

Real and Fake News

Washington is a town obsessed with the latest news. Owing to the political power invested in the capitol city, what happens in the media is treated very seriously and often becomes part of the dynamic that moves legislation and leads to official government action. People angle to be on national television and prominent news websites because those conversations become part of the storyline that shapes official decisions.

Yet the news media have changed in fundamental respects. The rise of the internet has created new online platforms that look and act like conventional news sources but are highly partisan and have widely varying standards. Some conform to the goals of traditional news organizations, whereas others spread lies, foster conspiracy theories, and propagate myths to large numbers of people.

At a time when democracy is teetering on the edge, new outlets alter the information ecosystem and add considerable risks to the political system. Media coverage is more personal and sensationalized, and it also tends to be more extreme and partisan. There are well-known differences in how various outlets cover the news. And there are internet websites that look just like conventional newscasters but are deeply political and closely aligned with specific ideological interests.

One has to be very careful in dealing with media outlets because contemporary reporters are often evaluated based on the number of pageviews they generate. If you are part of a story that goes viral, that is terrific for the individual reporter and their news organization, but it is generally not good for you. There can be coverage that damages you as a large number of people tweet and retweet the sensationalized headlines. One has to avoid becoming "click bait" for reporters seeking to build their brands as anything that elevates online readership is fair game for enterprising writers.

Sometimes, the attacks came from the Left. One of my well-respected colleagues wrote a paper complaining about predatory practices and abusive market behavior by large technology firms and the need for a new digital regulatory agency to oversee these companies. At a time of a growing techlash against the sector, there was clearly a need for stronger enforcement actions against large firms. The paper was a well-researched and well-written explanation of how that should happen.

Against that backdrop, it was surprising when the *American Prospect*, a leading liberal organ, attacked the paper as pro-industry.[38] Its writer noted that Brookings had accepted contributions from companies and ignored the author's critical stance on the tech sector and his recommendation that it was time to create a new agency to regulate those companies. It was an "Alice in Wonderland" argument where up was down, and a paper that made the case for stiffer regulation was seen as favorable to tech companies. To me, the attack was misplaced because the paper's author had written a tough-minded piece that was hard on the industry.

Outsiders loved to take our work out of context and criticize it. As an example, I once wrote a blog post on twenty-one questions that members of Congress should ask tech CEOs when they were testifying before Congress. The items included questions such as, "Have you hired ethicists to help you design products and think about the societal ramifications of your technologies? Do you believe the California Consumer Privacy Act is a good model for the nation to adopt and would you encourage members of Congress to pass legislation modeled on that bill? How have you diversified your corporate leadership team and your company workforce, and what are the current breakdowns for your company as a whole by race, gender, ethnicity, and U.S. states where employees work? and What have you done to stop the use of your products for racist appeals, hateful actions, or false information?"[39]

Yet, when writing his critique, the author ignored these entreaties and said that my asking, "What is your greatest hope about technology today?" proved I was anti-consumer despite years of pro-consumer writings in books and articles. In his column, there was no mention of the other twenty questions and their efforts to elicit meaningful information from the executives. That approach was often par for the course because in a world of tweets and sensationalized headlines, it was easy to pick one sentence out of a blog post and condemn people based on that snippet. Critics knew no one would read the longer report and understand it was an unsubstantiated accusation.

Occasionally, prominent politicians used the news media to go after specific organizations. For example, Senator Bernie Sanders criticized the centrist Third Way for its supposed ties to Wall Street Democrats, and he complained that "they want us to go back to their failed corporate approach, which has led to a massive level of income and wealth inequality, a bloated military budget and a failure to address the crises of climate change, a broken criminal justice system and inhumane immigration policies."[40]

Senator Elizabeth Warren did the same thing against Brookings when she condemned a paper about financial services written by one of our nonresident scholars, Bob Litan. She pointed to his support from a mutual fund and claimed that the support led to biased research. In a letter, she said the report was "highly compensated and editorially compromised work on behalf of an industry player seeking a specific conclusion."[41]

Brookings responded by saying that his paper was written "in his private capacity, not connected with Brookings in any way." After investigating the situation, though, the think tank's leadership didn't fault Litan for his research but criticized him for a failure to comply with a new internal rule on congressional testimony that prohibited nonresident scholars from using their Brookings affiliation. Even though Litan said he was not aware of the institution's new requirement, Brookings got him to resign.[42]

That quelled Warren's ire but unleashed outrage about Brookings's lack of support for Litan's academic freedom. Some scholars inside the institution felt the move was the equivalent of a "jaywalking" offense. A number believed the organization capitulated to Warren over fear of alienating a powerful Democratic senator, not that Litan had done anything seriously wrong other than state his personal policy views, which scholars felt was protected by the institution's commitment to academic freedom.

Several years later, Brookings redressed the injustice by reinstating his nonresident senior fellow position and publishing one of his books. He wrote thoughtful pieces for us and I spoke at his book launch as a sign of solidarity with him. The speed of his initial termination had shocked many people, but bringing him back allowed Litan to continue his work.

Sometimes reporters went after their fellow writers. There was critical coverage involving David Brooks of the *New York Times* after he launched an Aspen Institute activity called Weave: The Social Fabric Project. It was financed by Facebook and involved him authoring a short blog post on Facebook's corporate site extolling the virtues of Groups, a tool for online communities. He furthermore spoke at a video conference organized by New York University where a Facebook-funded paper was released.

Media critics lambasted him for not disclosing the funding relationship with the tech giant, and Aspen for working so closely with the company.[43] After initial reporting by *BuzzFeed News*, the *Washington Post* picked up the story and rebuked Brooks for not publicly disclosing the funding. It accused him of violating journalistic ethics by not informing his readers of the corporate funding while writing pieces that praised Facebook's online platform.[44] In short order, Brooks resigned his position leading the Aspen Institute project.[45]

Foreign Issues

A number of Brookings leaders have argued that key parts of the future lie in China, and scholars should spend as much time as possible there to understand that country. Brookings president Strobe Talbott was a committed globalist who had served as deputy secretary of state in the Clinton State Department. He had been Bill Clinton's roommate at Oxford University and had an enviable network of international contacts. He wanted our scholars to broaden their focus beyond America to learn from and work with other countries.

Yet those decisions about spending more time in China turned out to be trickier than previously imagined. Rather than a rosy scenario featuring shared prosperity and common economic interests between China and the United States, geopolitics were shifting, and forces were developing within America that would openly attack China and see it as a major economic competitor and security threat. Any organization that did work there could become a casualty of the rapidly moving alignments.

Similar tensions were arising in other parts of the world. Countries that were considered U.S. allies at one point in time could become problematic at another point in time. If there were projects underway when the tide turned, it could expose scholars to criticisms for working in a nation that was viewed with suspicion, even if there were shared diplomatic and defense agreements with those countries.

One of our international units had started a relationship with Saudi Arabia based on an ambitious development plan there known as Vision 2030. A young prince known as Mohammad bin Salman (also known as MBS) had put together a plan to diversify the Saudi economy and bring reforms to the kingdom. He claimed his goal was to bring his country into the twenty-first century and modernize its archaic practices, including allowing women to drive cars and own property.

But after that effort launched, something happened that dramatically changed people's views about Saudi Arabia. In 2018, a Saudi critic named Jamal Khashoggi visited the Saudi consulate office in Istanbul in order to get a visa. His fiancé was waiting outside the building but Khashoggi never came out. For days, it was unclear what had happened, and Saudi officials denied any wrongdoing.

However, slowly details emerged that revealed a vicious murder. A Saudi team is said to have tortured, killed, and dismembered Khashoggi, and Turkish officials claimed they had secret recordings of the gruesome death scene. Further investigation alleged that several members of the assassination squad belonged to MBS's personal bodyguard. The Crown Prince denied any personal involvement, but the world was outraged by the treacherous and bloody action. There were months of negative coverage of Saudi Arabia that asked how any country's leadership could undertake such horrific deeds.[46]

It wasn't long before reporters turned to the many prominent universities and think tanks that had worked with the Saudis. How could they take money from such a vicious regime, even if it was an ally of the United States? Were they siding with murderers and assassins, journalists wondered out loud? In short order, Brookings and several universities renounced their Saudi funding. That action was clearly the right thing to do given the vicious act that had occurred.

Other think tanks were enduring similar scrutiny over their foreign activities. The Council on Foreign Relations garnered negative press when it hosted a Zoom webinar moderated by CNN's Fareed Zakaria that featured Javad Zarif, the foreign minister of Iran. The *Washington Free Beacon* called him "Iran's chief propagandist" and suggested that the forum violated U.S. sanctions against that country. It cited a U.S. State Department spokesperson who argued "considering the Iranian regime's brutal execution of Navid Afkari on Saturday, no country or organization should be giving Foreign Minister Zarif a platform to spread his propaganda. Zarif and his government should only be met with isolation and censure for their barbarity."[47] The Council on Foreign Relations defended the event by saying that "canceling would establish a precedent and a standard that could preclude us hosting officials from a significant number of countries" and pointed out that hosting a forum with a foreign official did not constitute an endorsement of him or his country's policies.

The Atlantic Council engendered criticism over its relationship with Turkey, even though that country was allied with the United States and was part of the North Atlantic Treaty Organization. As that government turned more authoritarian under the leadership of President Tayyip Erdoğan, the think tank was accused of serving as a "PR arm of the Turkish government." It raised money from the Turkish government and had executive committee members who were registered foreign agents of other nations. Its program on Ukraine received financial support from the natural gas company sector, even though its leading scholar in that area expressed "uneasiness" about the relationship.[48]

Brookings also had a long relationship with Turkey. It was a country that previously had been democratic and a strong partner of the United States. But over time, it had turned illiberal and imprisoned thousands of its own people. Their main infraction seemed to be a willingness to speak out against the country's antidemocratic tendencies.

One day, what had previously been a human rights dispute turned into an ugly confrontation between protestors and security guards for President Erdoğan. Well before his regime's turn to illiberalism, he had been invited to speak at Brookings. He attracted a large crowd of people outside the building, who were unhappy with the tenor of his regime. When the protesters shouted attacks on his policies, Erdoğan's guards waded into the crowd right outside our building and assaulted the dissidents.[49] The Turkish security personnel also sought to prevent critical journalists from attending our open event, something that forced our institution's president to go out and personally escort individual reporters into our auditorium. It was a wild scene that had escalated quickly.

The outrageous behavior led to soul-searching about when and under what circumstances we should allow illiberal leaders to speak at Brookings. For years, we had prided ourselves on being open to a variety of speakers and being eager to engage major leaders from other nations that did not share our democratic values. Yet the rise of thuggish behavior from some of these governments put that approach under tremendous pressure. We did not want to appear to be siding with antidemocratic leaders who openly attacked dissidents and tried to keep reporters from covering public speeches.

To make sure no one missed the point about the contentious foreign environment, the U.S. State Department three weeks before the 2020 election announced a new policy by which think tanks and universities had to disclose their foreign government funding in order to engage with its officials. "To protect the integrity of civil society institutions, the Department requests henceforth that think tanks and other foreign policy organizations that wish to engage with the department disclose prominently on their websites funding they receive from foreign governments, including state-owned or state-operated subsidiary entities," Secretary of State Mike Pompeo announced. "Department staff will be mindful of whether disclosure has been made and of specific funding sources that are disclosed when determining whether and how to engage."[50] This was not a problem at Brookings because we disclosed our donors, but not all think tanks and universities were doing that.

Despite unfounded accusations about cozying up to illiberal regimes, Brookings scholars were at the forefront of standing up for liberal democracy at home and opposing countries abroad that were backsliding away from freedom and personal liberty. There were numerous books and articles written showing our experts' support for liberal democracy, personal freedom, and human rights.

An example of our writing was on Hungary, which represented a case of illiberal democracy that appeared to be sliding into authoritarianism. Our experts regularly condemned that regime and documented its antidemocratic actions. Several who wrote on the topic cited Hungary as a poster boy for illiberal rule. But whenever our scholars wrote those critical pieces, there would be calls from the Hungarian ambassador or his staff saying our critiques were unfair and demanding the right to publish something on the Brookings website rebutting our analysis. Each time one of our experts stated that Hungary was moving away from democracy, its embassy officials would deny the charge and demand the right of rebuttal.

The Hungarians were remarkably persistent in asking for something we would never grant, and they seemed to think that if they repeated their protestations long enough regarding our criticism of their illiberalism, nobody would think they were undemocratic.[51] It was an unwarranted stance on their part, but their officials were quite vocal in expressing their unhappiness with our characterizations of their political system.

Throughout all these skirmishes over money, impeachment, media coverage, and geopolitics, it was clear that both America and the world in general were changing in ominous ways. As someone who had been an academic for forty years, I could see the ways in which personal risks were rising and that the political vicissitudes facing civil society were intensifying. Day-to-day life in a think tank as well as in universities was becoming a powder keg that could go off at any time. Changes in the media ecosystem were increasing the risks, and the political challenges associated with money, ultranationalism, and authoritarianism were rising. There were many days over the last decade when I was terrified regarding the numerous things that could go wrong for Brookings, me, and the country.

7

Personal Investigations

Political attacks can come from a variety of different sources as there is widespread resentment against the power of the capitol city. Everyone can cite examples of politicians who ran against the capitol city and then got "Potomac fever" and never left. They become lobbyists, behind the scenes power brokers, or influence peddlers who put their names at the service of major economic or political interests.

At the same time, there is a widespread perception that D.C. residents are unrepresentative and self-interested. While elites in the capitol city have flourished, many people in the rest of the country have not done well economically. Most workers have not seen a meaningful improvement in their livelihoods since the 1980s. Public policy has tilted in favor of corporate interests and wealthy individuals, with tax cuts going to the rich while the costs of education, health care, and housing have soared.

There are many reasons for these trends, but a number of individuals from outside D.C. see the leaders there as not having served the national interest. That viewpoint has generated considerable public resentment and anger, and made news reporters, media commentators, think tank experts, and thought leaders inviting targets for political leaders who play on citizen mistrust and resentment.

Deep State

Trump capitalized on negative perceptions about the capitol city by characterizing opponents as members of a secretive, deep state. Rather than trying to bring people together to deal with failed trade policies and the loss of economic opportunity, he divided people from one another, castigated his critics, and labeled opponents as corrupt and dishonest. He questioned people's motives and sought to undermine dissident voices. He used the bully pulpit of the presidency to discourage anyone from speaking out against him.

Sharp criticisms from him were especially pronounced during his presidency, which made it a particularly risky time in D.C. The New York billionaire had won the presidency by telling the country that East Coast elites were not trustworthy. According to him, those individuals had lined their own pockets at the expense of everyone else. They had negotiated trade deals that shipped jobs first to Mexico and then to China and elsewhere in Asia. Privileged elites had opened borders that brought immigrants who competed with Americans for many jobs. In his eyes, they were responsible for the weak economic opportunities in middle America.

Trump challenged the loyalty of national officials and accused them of being unpatriotic Americans. Ditto for the intelligence community, technical experts, and inspectors general, whose jobs were to make sure federal money was being well spent and policies followed. When they issued critical reports, it wasn't because their conclusions were based on the facts but because the analysts hated Trump and would do everything in their power to tear him down.

In press briefings, Trump showed open disdain for reporters

from many mainstream news organizations and incited his supporters to believe the press was completely unfair and totally against
him. He singled out individual reporters for snide comments, such
as "you are fake" and "you work for a fake organization." Any reporter who deigned to ask a critical question or wrote in a skeptical
vein became a target of the president's wrath. Since Trump thought
he was doing a spectacular job, his anger grew to include many of
the people who worked in D.C.

His strategy represented a powerful way to delegitimize the
media sector whose major task was to hold leaders accountable. As
argued by writer and broadcaster Marvin Kalb, if the press was seen
as the "enemy of the people," no one would take their criticisms seriously.[1] Rather than believing reporters were making sincere efforts
to question his statements, journalists were increasingly seen as
partisan players, which negated their ability to question leadership
decisions and hold leaders accountable.

Confronting Higher Education

Educational institutions are under attack as well. The U.S. Department of Justice under Trump investigated a number of universities
for what it said was a failure to disclose financial support from foreign sources. Most schools garnered a considerable amount of non--
U.S. funding so the federal probes created quite a chill. University
officials worried the worsening political environment would harm
academic exchanges and international cooperation.

A West Virginia University professor was charged with hiding
his work with China's Thousand Talents Plan while he was on sab-
batical. The Plan is a Chinese government initiative that recruits
researchers to work on research projects with Chinese academics.
The U.S. Department of Justice has targeted those projects as part
of its "China Initiative" against foreign espionage. The attorney who

investigated the case defended this prosecution saying, "We're not attacking universities. These things are often very sophisticated, without university knowledge or other industry knowledge."[2]

However, lawyers defending academic clients complained that government rules were unclear. "If you're a scientist, you are not probably that much into paperwork and you don't really fully understand the rules. You're doing your best to disclose, but you didn't get training from universities or federal agencies, you get very limited training, and you're doing your best to comply," noted attorney Catherine Pan-Giordano.

Attorneys for a Harvard professor, Charles Lieber, arrested for hiding Chinese funding, filed a breach of contract lawsuit against the university. The complaint argued, "Harvard acted solely in its own self-interest by turning its back on a dedicated faculty member." Although the university accepted $10 million in Chinese research money that Charles Lieber brought in, his lawyers said the university "left Professor Lieber in the lurch seeking to distance itself from him through denial of his advancement and indemnification requests."[3]

A University of Tennessee engineering professor was indicted for not revealing a part-time position with the Beijing University of Technology. Federal government grant applications now require information on foreign employment, and prosecutors alleged that the faculty member had not done that. However, a jury failed to convict him after the instructor provided evidence that on several occasions he had notified the university of his Chinese employment, in writing.[4]

Political pressures also intensified through probes of American universities that set up Confucius Institutes promoting Chinese language and culture.[5] A number of places, such as Duke University, Indiana University, the University of Chicago, and the University of Maryland, among others, opened such programs, which were financed by gifts of more than $250,000 from the Chinese Ministry of Education. They supported language instruction and courses on Chinese history and culture. At their peak, dozens of American universities hosted Confucius Institutes.[6]

But over the last few years, these institutes have come under attack due to the connection with the Chinese government. Critics challenged China's poor human rights record, lack of respect for academic freedom, and surveillance of Chinese students, and said universities should not be cooperating with China. To put force into that edict, Congress in 2019 enacted a law to the effect that universities could not have funding both from the U.S. Department of Defense and for Confucius Institutes. After that, most American universities closed their institutes for fear of jeopardizing their military support.[7]

Federal Investigations

If legislation did not get universities' attention, the U.S. Department of Education under Trump surely did when it launched investigations into higher education's disclosure compliance. In letters to Georgetown University, Texas A&M University, and many other leading institutions, the agency requested years of data regarding foreign gifts to see if these schools were disclosing support raised from abroad.[8]

When the results were released two weeks before the 2020 election, the department proclaimed in big, bold headlines that universities were guilty of "vast underreporting of foreign gifts." It cited schools that had not reported over $6.5 billion in contributions from China, Qatar, Russia, Saudi Arabia, and United Arab Emirates, among others. In promoting its report, Secretary Betsy DeVos warned that "the threat of improper foreign influence in higher education is real. Our action today ensures that America's students, educators, and taxpayers can follow the money."[9]

Having an open educational system has always been seen as a valuable strength of higher education. In the contentious contemporary environment, though, professors and universities are being attacked for activities that had previously been encouraged. Just a few years earlier, universities wanted faculty to work with foreign schools and seek external funding from foreign sources. It was part of the university globalization that many educational leaders openly espoused.[10]

But in the new political environment, anything connected with China or certain other nations was viewed with suspicion. Even co-authoring scientific articles with Chinese researchers was coming under attack. A Hoover Institution report from Stanford University complained about U.S. publications with experts at seven Chinese universities and institutes, and suggested the American scientists involved in the writing were directly or indirectly aiding the Chinese military. Even though the U.S. academics had violated no laws, the report claimed that they were aiding the enemy.[11]

As the United States increased its vigilance toward Chinese scholars operating in America, China pushed back hard. It felt that Americans were getting too tough on its experts. One of its leading media executives warned that American arrests of Chinese scientists was "not good . . . [for the] safety of some U.S. nationals in China."[12] The clear implication was a coming tit for tat crackdown on U.S. experts.

Against this backdrop of rising tensions between the countries, some U.S. media outlets took a tough line on Chinese connections, even if they only involved jointly organized conferences. A right-wing news website called the Washington Free Beacon took this stance when it accused scholars at the Brookings Doha Center of spying for the Chinese government through a partnership with the Shanghai Academy of Social Sciences. In 2018, the Doha director had signed a formal agreement with the Chinese think tank to hold two public conferences on international relations between China and the Middle East. Although international convenings were common between universities and Chinese think tanks, the conservative outlet blasted out the provocative headline, "Brookings Institution Partnered with Shanghai Policy Center under Scrutiny for Spying."[13]

The article claimed that the Chinese organization was "a front for China's intelligence and spy recruitment operations" and, in an effort to damage Joe Biden's presidential candidacy, noted that several of my colleagues were serving as informal advisers to his campaign. It was the ultimate "guilt-by-association" and a sign of the Joseph McCarthy–like atmosphere that was creeping into the D.C. scene. Making sure no one missed the insinuation, the reporter quoted a former adviser to the late defense secretary Donald Rumsfeld saying, "A lot of the think tanks are populated by former government officials who have inside information on how the government works, particular policies. They have connections to people who are still in the government, so they're a wealth of potential information."[14]

Private Investigators

For many years, law firms and political campaigns have employed private investigators to compile information on election opponents. The idea was that if you could find incriminating material on an opposition candidate that could be leaked to the press, it would help your candidacy and create serious problems for the opponent. There are numerous examples of politicians ruined by scandals that dashed their candidacies and destroyed their political futures.

Now these tools are being deployed against civil society leaders. If you are a business executive, a university administrator, a think tank expert, or a nonprofit leader, private investigators can look at your background, go through your garbage, interview those around you, and compile confidential data. There is a booming market for "data brokers" and "private spies" who purchase information from commercial enterprises regarding your income, expenditures, loans, homeownership, geolocation data, cable viewing habits, magazine subscriptions, and social media profiles, among other things.

In the digital world, there also are surreptitious tools that can dive deep into your personal life. If you use wi-fi at a hotel, restaurant, or coffee shop, it is easy to intercept your communications and see your texts and emails. Off-the-shelf software enables even amateur sleuths to gain access to many of the things that appear on your computer screen.

Furthermore, people posing as reporters, documentary filmmakers, or security agents can entrap ordinary individuals into revealing private information, even though the person doesn't realize those individuals are investigators who wish to harm particular subjects. It is a Wild West of information brokerage and personal entrapment that can lure unsuspecting victims into harm's way.

In a book entitled *Spooked*, former *New York Times* investigative reporter Barry Meier reveals the widespread use of private investigators to sabotage opponents.[15] Using the shadowy networks of former law enforcement and security specialists, there are firms that focus on intelligence-gathering and data collection, and he demonstrates through numerous cases how the explosion of digital information creates considerable risks for anyone defined as a target. In today's world, few are safe from determined adversaries who want confidential material.

When compromising information is uncovered, it is leaked to friendly reporters, who use this material to write scathing exposés on the targeted individual. Sheltering media sources through the cloak of anonymity, they use confidentially gained information to report on spending, lifestyles, private conversations, personal relationships, or social media proclivities. If you ever wrote a tweet that was profane, unpolitic, rude, or directed at a powerful opponent, it can be used against you.

At other times, material is turned over to congressional or executive branch investigators to be used for partisan purposes. As national politics has polarized, government investigations have become more partisan in nature. Some congressional committee lawyers are people who use confidential information to attack those who have a point of view that differs from particular legislators. Without even being aware, you can get caught in partisan crossfires that damage your career.

This unholy alliance between private spies, journalists, and congressional investigators creates grave risks for thought leaders. The people who collect this information are sheltered by the cloak of press anonymity and committee investigations. Anonymous sources mean the object of the attack will likely have no idea who sabotaged them. The culprit can commit the ambush without the source's identity ever being revealed, making it about as close to a perfect crime as can occur today.

The most concrete way of protecting your civil liberties during illiberal times is having experienced and knowledgeable lawyers. Skilled attorneys can ward off attacks, limit investigations, challenge unfair tactics, question subpoenas, criticize prosecution tactics, go public to the media, and guard against selective enforcement of the rules. In the worst-case scenario, it is crucial to have legal representation that defends against partisan attacks, overly broad subpoenas, tainted investigations, or unfair prosecutions. The problem, however, is that not everyone can afford top-notch counsel, some of whom charge hundreds or thousands of dollars per hour.

Challenging Activities

Georgetown parties used to be the most desired invitations in Washington, D.C. They were the place where the wealthy and powerful gathered to compare notes and curry favor with those in a position to offer political help. The stately homes with high ceilings and vintage furniture provided a great setting for free-flowing conversation and power deals.

But over the years, alternatives rose to take the place of Georgetown gatherings. There were dinners sponsored by media outlets, corporations, or foundations that featured experts explaining current controversies and how they should be addressed. And there were events Brookings held that brought together people from government, business, academia, and the nonprofit sector around important substantive topics.

At these events, you had to be careful what you did or said. About a decade ago, Brookings was accused of misbehavior in an article that discussed how our scholars raised money from foreign governments and supposedly connected those officials to U.S. leaders. The story focused on Norway, alleged a scholar had facilitated meetings between officials in the two countries, and quoted lawyers who claimed this represented a violation of the Foreign Agents Registration Act.[16]

That legislation had been enacted just before World War II when there was concern about German-based Nazis influencing American policy, and as a result, legislators created disclosure requirements for representation of foreign governments. If you represented a foreign government, you had to register as a foreign agent (or as a lobbyist for a foreign entity) and publicly disclose information regarding those ties.

The article set off shock waves within the institution because the story appeared on the front pages of a leading national newspaper and had emails and accounts of personal meetings that the reporters believed buttressed their critique of our activities. Our lawyers rebutted the claims and argued that Brookings was an academic institution that did not lobby and was not in violation of the legal provisions.

But we took the allegation seriously and held a number of meetings to revise our policies and institute protections designed to ensure that we stayed on the right side of the law as well as widely accepted ethical standards. As we had done for many years, Brookings disclosed its donors and published an annual report that listed our trustees and donors, and what they gave. We also instituted mandatory ethics training for employees so people understood the rules.

In addition, every fundraising proposal was reviewed by multiple lawyers, communications experts, and administrators in our executive office to make sure it conformed to institutional policies. Before any money could be raised, there were reviews to make sure we were not engaging in lobbying, that scholars abided by our conflict of interest rules, and that our work was independent in nature. We took these commitments to heart and rejected any money that came with strings attached. We recognized the very credibility of our work depended on people's trust and confidence in our research.

In a polarized time, though, external critics were sometimes hard to satisfy. Trump supporters regularly attacked our scholars and research. They used ultraconservative websites or media outlets to condemn Brookings. One day, after a national outlet complained about one of our scholars, a colleague mentioned the fact that she had just been denounced by a prominent news organization. I commented that it was nothing new and that during the 2020 campaign, our colleagues were getting denounced all the time by external forces. "What is a day without a denunciation?" another individual joked.

But the condemnations were not a laughing matter. The attacks on knowledge sector experts and independent research were becoming a routine part of the political landscape. To reduce the fodder for external complaints, we made sure that the events we organized were consistent with the research our scholars were doing. We invited distinguished experts from universities, agencies, and nonprofit organizations to participate in our events to ensure that multiple points of view were represented. And in our writings, what we published went through a rigorous review process. Despite those efforts to safeguard our work, it remained quite challenging to operate within such a supercharged and highly polarized environment.

Anti-Semitism

The shifting geopolitics sometimes turned very ugly and exposed scholars to personal attacks. In his analysis of Eastern European autocracies, Brookings expert Norm Eisen explains how authoritarian rulers have a step-by-step approach of prosecuting professors, criticizing opposition politicians, undermining journalists, and packing the courts with sycophantic judges. He later updated this with an analysis of risks for U.S. democracy.[17] Academics who had previously been sheltered in the ivory tower are seeing growing dangers from their external involvements as the world of ideas is no longer insulated from domestic politics and international affairs.

Rather than applauding his support for democratic rules, conservatives cynically used Eisen's playbook against him by saying that he was a liberal who was trying to orchestrate an Eastern European–style coup against President Donald Trump. Appearing on the widely watched Fox News Tucker Carlson television show, Darren Beattie of the Revolver website accused Eisen of employing "an engineered contested election combined with mass mobilization protests" to take down Trump, similar to the "color revolutions" that had unfolded in Ukraine, the Czech Republic, and elsewhere. Beattie cited my colleague's analysis of Eastern European dictators to claim that Eisen was part of a liberal conspiracy to overthrow Trump. Beattie called him a "hatchet man" who was the "key architect to censor, sue, impeach, and overthrow the President."[18]

Because these claims were made on a prime-time television show that attracted millions of viewers each night, there was an outpouring of calls, online comments, and tweets attacking Eisen. Several individuals openly threatened him with bodily harm while others resorted to outright anti-Semitism. On the Revolver site following the article on Eisen, a person claimed "the coup against Trump was correctly labeled a 'Jew coup' by Rick Wiles of *TruNews*" and complained that "every other media outlet is owned and controlled by filthy fucking Jews." Other shocking comments criticized Eisen as "another Jew who hates the United States. Will people now realize that the Jews are not our friends and they are neck deep in funding every left wing progressive group in this country?"[19]

These anti-Semitic pronouncements represented dramatic indications of the ugliness undergirding America during this highly polarized era. Scholars seeking to understand and analyze global developments could be whipsawed into public controversies and portrayed as un-American or security threats themselves. At a time where power swings quickly from liberal to conservative and back again, and each side has very different views regarding policy and political issues, the personal and professional dangers are high.

8

Social Shaming

In 2020, TechFreedom president Berin Szoka was forced to step down after he tweeted "serious question: could there possibly [be] any greater poetic justice in the universe than for Trump to die of the #CPACvirus?"[1] For his inappropriate speculation, the technology policy organization removed him from its leadership position.

Journalist Wesley Lowery was rebuked by *Washington Post* executive editor Marty Baron for a tweet that described people at a D.C. book event as "decadent aristocrats." The executive wrote Lowery an official reprimand that accused him of "failing to perform your job duties by engaging in conduct on social media that violates the *Washington Post*'s policy and damages our journalistic integrity. We need to see immediate cessation of [your] improper use of social media, outlined above. Failure to address this issue will result in increased disciplinary action, up to and including the termination of your employment."[2]

Later, a memo from Baron to the paper's staff expressed the editor's concern about social media damaging journalistic integrity. "The *Post* is more than a collection of individuals who wish to express themselves. The reputation of the *Post* must prevail over any one individual's desire for expression," he wrote.[3] His admonition reflected the sentiment of an old-school executive troubled by the open and unfiltered expression emerging online among some of his younger writers.

Yet it also demonstrated a recognition of how social media can be a problematic venue. It is a "dual-use" technology that can be employed for good such as by promoting creative work to large numbers of people. But Twitter and Facebook can also be cesspools where vile commentary is prevalent, emotional reactions are typical, and the fury of the mob can descend quickly from either the Left or the Right.

As noted by Sheera Frenkel and Cecilia Kang in their book, *An Ugly Truth: Facebook's Battle for Domination*, social media connect the world, but they have also been "mishandling users' data, spreading fake news, and amplifying dangerous, polarizing hate speech." The result has been "inflammatory rhetoric, conspiracy theories, and partisan filter bubbles."[4] In a similar vein, Anne Applebaum and Peter Pomerantsev complain that "our democratic habits have been killed off by an internet kleptocracy that profits from disinformation, polarization, and rage."[5]

Rise of Social Media

Twitter is an unforgiving place that trolls reporters, politicians, celebrities, and experts and unleashes emotional condemnations on targeted individuals. It is easy to incite a tsunami of online hatred— short phrases or sentences taken out of context can make someone look bad and encourage others to call for the person's resignation.

The interaction of social media platforms with political polarization and extremism means tweets are risky, and vilification can come quickly, widely, and intensely. With the limitation on the number of characters, Twitter encourages brevity, taking things out of context,

and instant reaction. Sometimes, when I am about to react to a headline on a news story, the platform now asks me whether I want to
READ the article before I post a response. That is always a useful
reminder that there may be more nuance in a posting than reflected
by what others are saying about it. False impressions are easy to
reach, and it is surprisingly common for people to misinterpret important developments.

Misunderstandings are rampant on many different issues. In
2019, there was a highly visible illustration of public venom when
some young kids visiting from Coventry Catholic High School in
Kentucky toured the Lincoln Memorial following a March for Life
rally. With its expansive views of the Mall, not to mention its obvious
historic interest, the spot was a popular gathering place for many
groups. People went to visit the tourist site, express their political
views, or engage in spirited protests.

As the young students stood on the steps of the Lincoln Memorial, they encountered a Native American veteran, Nathan Phillips,
who had attended an Indigenous peoples' rally and was playing a
drum. Some of the boys were wearing Trump's "Make America
Great Again" hats, and videos from the episode initially made it look
like they were taunting the elderly man.

When the video went viral, accompanied by a narrative of youth-
ful disrespect, the social media reaction was instantaneous. The
young boys were portrayed as being disrespectful of Native Americans and denying Phillips his basic rights of political expression.
They were condemned personally, and their high school apologized
for their students' poor behavior and launched an investigation with
the threat of expelling them from school and thereby derailing their
graduation and possible college plans. The entire episode was used
to illustrate the point that young, conservative white men were rude
and intolerant, and just one more example of how Trump was inciting hatred in America.

However, as more videos came to light, there were important ad-
ditions to the narrative. Right before the young men had encountered

Phillips, they had been accosted by a group of young Black men who were adherents of a fringe organization known as Hebrew Israelites. That group had shouted racist slurs at the Native Americans and directly confronted the Coventry youth. In an effort to deal with the racist chants, these young men had launched their own chant as a way to drown out the incendiary comments of the other group. Rather than disrespecting Phillips, as media accounts had initially suggested, they claimed they were trying to defuse a situation that had already escalated through the actions of others.[6]

Feeling aggrieved by the news coverage, one of the involved students, Nicholas Sandmann, filed a defamation lawsuit against outlets such as the *Washington Post*, CNN, the *New York Times*, CBS, and ABC, among others. He alleged that reporters had "targeted and bullied" him in an effort to "embarrass Trump." In regard to the *Washington Post*, the lawsuit argued, "The *Post* ignored basic journalist standards because it wanted to advance its well-known and easily documented, biased agenda against President Donald J. Trump by impugning individuals perceived to be supporters of the President." His attorneys suggested that the paper attacked the young man "because he was the white, Catholic student wearing a red 'Make America Great Again' souvenir cap." After some legal hearings, the *Post* settled the case out of court with a "mutually agreeable resolution."[7]

But the leader who took social media disparagement to new heights was clearly Trump. His "Twitter Presidency" drove news coverage, and until he was kicked off the platform, it gave him a personal tool with which to react instantly, condemn an opponent, or inflame the passions of his followers. The *New York Times* undertook an extensive analysis of his 11,390 tweets in the first two years of his presidency and found that 50 percent had attacked opponents, 20 percent had singled himself out for praise, and 10 percent had demanded action on issues of concern to him, notably on immigration and trade tariffs. The newspaper called Twitter "the broadcast network for Mr. Trump's parallel political reality" and a way to convey alternative facts, conspiracy theories, and false information.[8]

After accumulating tens of millions of followers before he was de-platformed for inciting violence, the former president used the social medium to dominate news coverage. His tweets were disseminated broadly and incorporated in legions of media stories. Even while they criticized him, reporters could not resist spreading his many statements and misleading comments.

Online Vitriol

High-profile cases demonstrate how pervasive online confrontation has become and how easy it is to provoke strong reactions. Some-times, casual comments or offhand tweets can land people in se-rious jeopardy. They may say or do something online that others object to and suffer job losses or adverse consequences.

A young data scientist named David Shor discovered this first-hand. Working for a company named Civis Analytics, Shor tweeted out an analysis by Princeton professor Omar Wasow, a well-respected scholar, regarding the electoral impact of violent versus nonviolent protest. Using Wasow's data analysis, Shor argued that "Post-MLK-assassination race riots reduced Democratic vote share in surrounding counties by 2%, which was enough to tip the 1968 election to Nixon. Non-violent protests 'increase' Dem vote, mainly by encouraging warm elite discourse and media coverage."[9]

In making this argument, Shor basically was saying Black Lives Matter protesters should heed the historic lesson of the 1960s and be aware that violent protests can generate voter backlashes that aid Republican candidates. In the aftermath of the George Floyd murder, he was seeking to present a respected Princeton scholar's empirical data that he felt were relevant to contemporary debates over political protests.[10]

Shortly after sending this tweet, though, progressive activists sharply rebuked Shor. Ari Trujillo Wesler of OpenField, a left-leaning app-maker, criticized him, saying, "This take is tone deaf, removes responsibility for depressed turnout from the 68 party, and reeks of anti-blackness." To make the point more emphatically, Wesler then contacted the chief executive officer of Shor's company and tweeted "come get your boy." The firm looked into the tweets and fired Shor. Contacted for his reaction, Shor said he had a non-disclosure agreement that prohibited him from publicly discussing his job termination.[11]

Even prominent Harvard University professors faced considerable risks in the contemporary environment. Professor Steven Pinker is a widely quoted author who has penned many books and articles. Yet 550 of his fellow linguists circulated a letter demanding that the Linguistics Society of America drop him as a distinguished fellow. They cited six tweets that he had posted over a six-year period and short phrases from his books. "Dr. Pinker has a history of speaking over genuine grievances and downplaying injustices, frequently by misrepresenting facts, and at the exact moments when Black and Brown people are mobilizing against systemic racism and for cruel changes," the signers argued. They said Pinker's use of phrases such as "urban crime" and "urban violence" represented racist codewords. The Harvard professor responded by criticizing his opponents as "speech police" and said they had "trolled through my writings to find offensive lines and adjectives."[12]

Unrepresentative Nature

Twitter is a place filled with opinionated people who respond rapidly to perceived injustices and are quick to condemn others. Online vitriol is common and widespread. One analysis of social platforms found that between 25 and 40 percent of U.S. internet users "say they have been harassed online" and that 57 percent of the abused are female.[13] It often does not take much to become the object of heated attacks. Indeed, some activists use the platform as a strategic weapon. After finding people who have engaged in objectionable behavior or rhetoric, they announce "Twitter, do your thing" and let a wave of public denunciations take the offender down.[14]

Online vilifying has been documented by the Anti-Defamation League. In a 2020 national survey, it found that "44% of Americans who responded to our survey said that they experienced online harassment." This was especially the case among marginalized Americans. Researchers found that "LGBTQ+ individuals, Muslims, Hispanics or Latinos, and African-Americans faced especially high rates of identity-based discrimination." A number indicated that they had also been victimized by stalking or physical threats.[15]

Abuses can happen from the Right or the Left because those who use Twitter and Facebook are unrepresentative of the general public. The former's users comprised just 22 percent of the country and tended to be much younger, more liberal, and more educated than the rest of the country. According to a Pew Research Center survey, 10 percent of tweeters generated 92 percent of the total tweets in the United States.[16]

In a news article, Axios chief executive officer Jim VandeHei described the problem this way: "Twitter is a mass-reality-distortion field for liberals and reporters. The group-think and liberal high-fiving [is] as bad as ever and continues to be a massive trap and distraction for journalists." And Facebook is little better. He noted, "[It] is a mass-reality-distortion field for conservatives. Look at the content pages that get the most daily interaction (shares, likes, etc.) and it's all right-wing catnip."

His bottom line was, "We're losing the war for truth," and social media platforms are a big part of the problem.[17] Rumors circulated quickly before any fact-checking could take place. Misleading statements would shape the public discourse even if they were based on obvious falsehoods or were taken out of context. Twitter speeded up the decisionmaking process within many organizations, and that sometimes led to very bad outcomes.

Personal Attacks

At Brookings, our high-profile scholars were frequent targets for rude, racist, or sexist comments. Some complaints moved beyond general insults to specific death threats, accompanied by home addresses and names of family members; that is, the threatener conveyed specific knowledge regarding where people actually lived. It was a time of heightened emotions, and some external critics viewed our experts not just as influential adversaries but as enemies to be defeated, publicly shamed, or killed.

My former colleague Susan Hennessey was on the receiving end of a critical tweet from conservative writer Mollie Hemingway, who was unhappy with that person's assertion that Russians had sought to help Trump win the 2016 election. Hemingway wrote, "This person and many of her colleagues should be held accountable for perpetuating the Russia collusion hoax with the help of their friends, the implicated officials. Their false claims damaged the country. There needs to be a reckoning." Susan responded by defending her analysis: "Mollie, there was no Russia collusion hoax. The IG [inspector general] found a properly predicated investigation. [Special Counsel] Mueller found a systematic plot by Russia to interfere in the US election, and that the president was aware of and sought to benefit from Russia's assistance while lying to the public."

When Susan was named to the national security division of the U.S. Department of Justice by President Joe Biden, opponents used her online exchanges to attack her. In a shocking turn, she became the object of a *Wall Street Journal* editorial entitled "A Dangerous Pick at Justice." The unsigned editorial board missive accused her of spreading lies over Twitter about Trump's Russia connections and said she sought to delegitimize Trump's 2016 presidential victory. It cited tweets, blog posts, and public commentary to buttress its case against her and said her appointment represented a sign that Biden and Attorney General Merrick Garland were moving away from "apolitical justice" and were shifting the department toward a dangerous partisanship.[18]

It was shocking to read this all-out assault on her personal integrity and expertise. When I had interviewed Susan for a job at Brookings, she struck me as incredibly smart, articulate, and insightful. She had graduated from Harvard Law School and worked at the National Security Administration. In everything she had done, she had impressed all the people she worked with from a variety of political persuasions. CNN hired her as an on-air national security expert, and I saw her on many occasions deliver incisive and fair-minded commentary on a wide range of topics.

Yet this unsigned attack from one of the nation's leading newspapers revealed she had powerful opponents. I never found out who wrote the piece or how it was published in such a high-profile outlet. But it appeared to be part of a coordinated campaign against her when the editorial critique was quickly tweeted by Senator Jon Cornyn of Texas, a conservative leader who was friends with President Trump. The former president's sympathizers were still smarting over their 2020 defeat and rushed to smear anyone who had taken a principled stance against his administration.

Scholar Ben Wittes was attacked on Twitter by Donald Trump Jr. after my colleague in the middle of the 2021 COVID pandemic tweeted an announcement regarding his own personal vaccination mandate policy, "I am with this tweet instituting my own vaccine mandate. I am not interacting with people any more whom I do not know to be vaccinated." Upon hearing this, the president's son angrily responded, saying, "No one gives a shit, but you win the Gold Medal for BS Twitter Virtue Signaling!"

I too became the object of indignant complaints, although not nearly in as visible a manner as my colleagues, who were on television all the time.[19] Following my publication of a short piece defending vote by mail procedures during the 2020 campaign, one man wrote me, "After reading your article claiming that unsolicited mail-in voting is party neutral, I had to fall on the floor laughing. Your claim is a lie and an absurdity, but then you are working for a leftist Democrat Party owned think tank that gets paid for publishing such drivel. I wonder what it feels like to go to bed at night knowing that your professional life is dedicated to publishing utter lies. . . . You and THE PARTY perpetuate this corruption because long ago your intellectual and moral rot became complete and permanent."

Another individual objected to a paper I wrote on why it is time to abolish the Electoral College. "It's pathetic that an old white man in the final years of his life wants to all of a sudden change the very foundation of our GREAT country. Why?? To let New York and California decide our Country's fate? I have no idea where you may reside or call home, I can only speculate that it is far, far away from the people you claim to represent," he argued.

Still another person left me a personal voicemail on my office phone saying I was "a piece of shit" for my analysis and asking me to call him so we could discuss the situation. I did not return his call because it seemed a conversation where my major objective would be to convince him I was not a piece of shit was not likely to be very productive.

After an op-ed I wrote complaining about COVID misinformation, someone else texted me this missive: "Newsflash, faggot—over half the country is refusing the vax. . . . You cannot force 100 million people to do anything at all. . . . The great news is that all you deep state boomer faggots will be dead soon of old age. Bye bye grandpa."

At other times, government officials went after those who made fun of them. Congressman Devin Nunes, for example, sued Twitter over two satirical sites @DevinCow and @DevinNunesMom, claiming they were defamatory in nature.[20] When a federal judge dismissed the lawsuit on freedom of speech grounds, his supporters were able to get the Trump Justice Department to issue a subpoena to Twitter so the legislator could see who had set up those accounts as well as another one known as @NunesAlt. This extraordinary use of federal investigative authority shocked both the social media firm and civil libertarians, who viewed the government subpoena as an unlawful abuse of legal tools. Twitter fought the request on grounds that it represented a federal overreach, and eventually the Justice Department withdrew the subpoena.[21]

That episode, though, demonstrated the lengths to which government departments could go to silence critics and intimidate opponents. It suggests the risky nature of the current contentious environment and how long-cherished freedoms are under threat from officials who want to limit freedom of expression. The perplexed operator of @NunesAlt plaintively asked "Why am I being sued by a US congressman? Why would the DOJ ever target me? Is it the mean tweets and bad memes?"[22]

During calmer times, it generally took a lot more than humorous parodies to get pursued by the Department of Justice, but these were not usual times. Not only did Trump's law enforcement department go after Twitter parody sites, the chief executive asked his Justice Department and the Federal Communications Commission to stop the NBC television show "Saturday Night Live" and other late night entertainment shows from teasing him. After SNL satirized him, he asked for action against the shows on grounds that "the 100% one-sided shows should be considered an illegal campaign contribution from the Democratic Party" and represented a violation of "equal time" requirements (even though the latter were eliminated in 1987).[23]

Social media platforms are so influential that they have become a vehicle for foreign espionage. Saudi Arabia infiltrated the Twitter workforce with secret agents tasked with getting confidential information about its critics. One of its agents employed at the firm was accused of "accessing thousands of user profiles without authorization to pass their identifying information—including phone numbers and IP addresses—reportedly to Bader al-Asaker, the head of

Saudi Crown Prince Mohammed bin Salman's charity and private office."[24] Along with another individual, they regularly sent confidential information to the Saudis about dissidents who anonymously used Twitter and were paid over $300,000, according to a federal indictment.

Zooming

Lots of mischief takes place via Zoom calls. Due to the COVID pandemic, everyone was forced to endure hours of video conference calls every day. What at first seemed a great convenience soon became a dreaded platform for many people. Even worse, its widespread use created security and safety loopholes that enterprising miscreants quickly exploited.

For example, a *Financial Times* reporter was suspended when he spied on internal calls from a competing news outlet, the *Independent*. According to company investigations, Mark DiStefano secretly logged in to the staff briefings from a private account and listened to his rival's conversations regarding staff furloughs and salary reductions via an audio feed. He then violated the organization's confidentiality by tweeting that secret news to his 100,000 followers, thereby stealing the thunder of the other newspaper.

A check of the Zoom log data, however, revealed that the unauthorized account was registered to DiStefano's *FT* email address. Christian Broughton, the editor of the *Independent,* put out a scathing media statement saying, "We respect freedom of speech and understand the challenges of news gathering, but the *Independent* considers the presence of a third-party journalist in a staff briefing to be entirely inappropriate and an unwarranted intrusion into our employees' privacy."[25]

Some video behaviors were much more egregious. Legal commentator Jeffrey Toobin was terminated after he masturbated during a *New Yorker* staff call. "I believed I was not visible on Zoom.

I thought no one on the Zoom call could see me. I thought I had muted the Zoom video," he explained. In what has to rank as the understatement of the year, he said it was an "embarrassingly stupid mistake."[26]

Even O. J. Simpson made fun at Toobin's expense when he joked "Daaaaamn, Jeffrey Toobin. At least, Pee-wee Herman was in an X-rated movie theater" when he engaged in that behavior.[27] Simpson clearly had a long memory concerning all the negative comments Toobin had expressed about him during his career as a prominent author and TV talking head. Others, however, defended Toobin on grounds that his behavior was private and hurt no one. "I don't like Twitter mobs, and I don't like bullies from the left or the right taking part in cancel culture," argued writer Jonathan Alter.[28]

Private group chats could be made public as well and can create trouble for the participants. In the midst of severe winter weather that paralyzed Texas power plants in 2021, Senator Ted Cruz and his wife Heidi generated an intense backlash when they left the state for a sunny Cancun vacation. At first, he blamed the trip on his two young daughters, saying it was their idea to avoid the frosty home-town temperatures without heat or electricity. But then someone leaked to the news media a confidential group chat with her neigh-bors and friends that showed Heidi complaining about the "FREEZ-ING" temperatures in Texas and extolling the low rates at the glitzy Ritz-Carlton hotel in the Mexican resort.[29]

Social and conventional news media sites went wild over the em-barrassing disclosures while comedians had a field day making fun of Senator Cruz's tone-deaf behavior. The Texan was not well liked by his political colleagues and thus provided an inviting target for others upset over his stunts and opportunistic behavior.

Being Vigilant

Through all these digital episodes, people had to be very vigilant about a wide range of online behaviors as the risky nature of Twitter, Facebook, Zoom, and other platforms reflect the changing character of mass communications. The proliferation of social media sites, video calls, tweets, and daily newsletters speeded up the news cycle and encouraged personalistic coverage. Established organs such as Politico report the latest information (Politico in its *Playbook* newsletter). Reaching several hundred thousand readers, *Playbook* is one of the Beltway's top outlets for summarizing the leading stories of the day and keeping influential people up to date on the latest developments. Mike Allen's *Axios AM* and *Axios PM* newsletters and *Punchbowl News* perform the same function and are widely read around the country.

One of *Playbook*'s more popular features is stories that track the comings and goings of prominent Washingtonians. For example, if you saw a senator in an airport, you can email the information to one of the newsletters to let others know that the individual was flying from D.C. to Atlanta and was sitting either in coach or in business class. People loved it when prominent government officials flew business class because it reinforced the public stereotype that they were entitled elites.

Pictures were even better. Once when Democratic senator Ron Wyden of Oregon was seen going to an airplane restroom with no shoes (considered gauche and unsanitary), a fellow traveler dutifully transmitted that nugget to Politico, which published it in the *Playbook*. The same thing happened to Senator Joe Manchin when he would go grocery shopping at the Waterfront Safeway. It was one of the reasons that it was useful not to be famous in D.C. The more prominent you were, the greater the odds of a random passerby reporting your idiosyncratic personal behavior to the press and trying to make you look silly.

It was a political era where firestorms could rage online over fictional depictions. For example, corporate donors reaped considerable criticism regarding financial support for a New York City Public Theater production of *Julius Caesar* that made a deranged Donald Trump the lead character. Conservative news sites had a field day complaining about the production's political message, and one audience member who attended the play was interviewed saying, "I didn't like that they made this person who looks like Trump get assassinated."

Artistic director Oscar Eustis defended the play on artistic grounds by arguing, "When we hold the mirror up to nature, often what we reveal are disturbing, upsettling, provoking things, Thank God, that's our job." Donald Trump Jr. raised questions about the play when he tweeted "I wonder how much of this 'art' is funded by taxpayers? Serious question, when does 'art' become political speech & does that change things?"[30] Faced with high-level pressure from the Trump family, some of the corporate donors pulled their funding from the theatrical production. Critics were momentarily mollified by this capitulation; sometimes, all it took was a concession like that to quiet the circling mob.

Risks of Rapid-Response Decisions

Within every organization, there are people who want a fast decision, prefer to rush through internal processes, or think "rapid response" is always the best way to proceed. Indeed, fast responses have become a common mantra in D.C. ever since presidential candidate Michael Dukakis erred in not responding to George Herbert Walker Bush's campaign attacks in 1988 and John Kerry let negative perceptions about his Vietnam War record go unanswered during August of the 2004 presidential campaign. The idea is that in a fast-moving political world, it is crucial to answer attacks, respond quickly, and make rapid decisions in order to prevent negative perceptions from turning public opinion against you or your organization.

In the social media world, the impetus to respond quickly is quite intense. Those skilled at crisis communications measure time in minutes or seconds, not hours or days. Tweets or online stories can be picked up fast and spread around the globe almost instantly so decisionmakers are under enormous pressure to react immediately before deep and immutable damage is incurred. Failure to respond rapidly is considered a cardinal sin by contemporary crisis managers.

Indeed, fast reactions have been internalized within many organizations. As noted by Adam Steinbaugh of the Foundation for Individual Rights in Education, "Administrations are conflict-averse. It doesn't really matter who is bringing up the complaints, they are eager to protect the reputation of the institution, protect the budget and avoid conflict."[31]

But this tendency creates unfortunate incentives for administrators because speed is often elevated over thoughtfulness or fairness. Many of the examples of unreasonable or imprudent decisions I witnessed in D.C. and elsewhere arose because of excessive speed that drove out reasoned responses. Sometimes, it is better to be deliberate and consult broadly than to make a quick decision that turns out to be wrong or to have unfair consequences for other people. The old adage of "speed kills" is a useful reminder to slow down when necessary and consider the ramifications of particular decisions. Instant decisionmaking during an era of social media is not always a wise process and can lead to gross unfairness and inequities.

9

Culture Wars

Observers used to describe the United States as a "melting pot" where people of diverse backgrounds came together, set aside their racial, ethnic, gender, and geographic differences, and saw one another as people united in a common purpose and identity. Of course, beneath the veneer, there were "subcultures" that flourished, and people were able to maintain particular identities. But a common interpretation decades ago was the unusual ability of Americans to overcome their demographic differences and work effectively together.[1]

Today, that vision seems completely outmoded. Many people don't want to melt and are eager to maintain their particular identities. They define themselves based on their backgrounds and life experiences, and they celebrate their distinctiveness from other individuals. As noted by Walter Benn Michaels, rather than coming together under a common rubric, they want their uniqueness to be acknowledged, and they want protection from those who don't respect their backgrounds.[2]

In this atmosphere, culture battles emerge over whose values should be appreciated, whose histories matter, and how to handle differences that emerge related to race, ethnicity, gender, age, religion, and personal lifestyle. Pitched arguments have unfolded over hot button issues ranging from wokism and cancel culture to microaggressions and critical race theory. People use these subjects to fight over cultural identity, organizational practices, and public policy. It is a period that inflames people of many different perspectives as the country struggles with the notion of what it means to be an American and how both contemporary as well as historical experiences should be handled.

Wedge Issues

In the current period, generational politics represent one of the cleavage points that percolate throughout the country. Despite legal prohibitions against age discrimination, the pejorative term "OK, Boomer" has become a common retort from Gen X and Zers frustrated at senior citizens in the workplace. In a critical book about the older generation, writer Helen Andrews complained that "the boomers, by clogging up the career pipeline, have refused to get off the stage. . . . Hopefully, the boomers will make a graceful exit and we can start seeing that soon, but if that doesn't work, then we are monumentally screwed."[3]

The polarized atmosphere created culture wars within many organizations and the country as a whole. People brought very different perspectives into the workplace, and administrators were forced to mediate a wide range of disputes. Some involved traditional issues, such as workload and job responsibilities, while in other cases disagreements arose based on personal background, life experiences, or governance questions.

Former president Trump and the people in his orbit complicated people's ability to address these differences. By being so open in his disdain for progressive young people, career-minded women, immigrants, and people of color, he poured fuel on divisions that existed within many places. He crystallized what was wrong with American society, yet made it difficult for those who opposed his views to get public and private organizations to resolve those issues.

During his presidency, we regularly dealt with the fallout from his rude statements, insensitive remarks, and wrong-headed policies. He would do something outrageous and dominate the public conversations. He would make people angry and lead them to demand clearcut actions that would confront him. He pushed many people to contest all the crazy things he was saying and doing.

In so doing, Trump followed a "wedge" strategy designed to divide liberals from moderates and drive opponents in a more extreme direction so that it would be easier to attack them for being out of the mainstream. He loved to characterize liberals as socialists and have opponents spend time arguing among themselves over how to respond to him as opposed to fighting the ultranationalist and noninclusive forces that were gaining power in middle America.

As various issues came up, we spent a lot of time debating possible remedies and how our experts should deal with Trump's initiatives. How should we respond to societal injustices, and should we move beyond research into more impactful actions? Opponents were organizing an all-out assault on American democracy and Republicans were using their party control of state legislatures in order to limit voting rights and they were utilizing the super-majority requirements of the U.S. Senate to stymie needed policy and political reforms. These individuals were quite unified, focused, and intentional in their strategy, while many moderates and progressives were disorganized, fragmented, and divided.

It was a classic "divide and conquer" approach that has often proven to be quite effective. Large groups get beaten by small entities that ruthlessly execute a highly targeted vision. There were many historic examples of small, unified forces winning surprising victories over larger but fractious majorities.

Few of our internal arguments were easy to resolve as people felt intensely about the rightness of their own positions.[4] As was true in many nonprofit organizations, we had a four-generation workforce in which twenty-two-year-olds were working side-by-side with those in their seventies and eighties, and it was not always easy to reconcile the differing expectations and viewpoints of these age groups.[5]

Yet, with the differing values and sensitivities of the various age groups, the atmosphere sometimes makes for tense dynamics. Public opinion surveys show that age matters a lot in individual viewpoints. As an illustration, young people are far more liberal in their political views than older people, and they are quite energetic in expressing their viewpoints.[6] One Pew Research Center poll found that 70 percent of Gen-Zers and 64 percent of millennials thought government should do more to solve problems, compared to only 49 percent of baby boomers and 39 percent of the silent generation.[7]

These differences popped up in all sorts of ways in our research, events, and individual interactions. I saw evidence of this with one of my colleagues who worked alongside young staffers. Over lunch with me one day, he raised the challenges of working in a multigenerational workplace. He noted that one of our colleagues was an impressive dresser and he wanted to tell her that "you look really good today," but he held himself back for fear his comment would be misconstrued as sexual harassment. He noted that MSNBC television anchor Chris Matthews had lost his job after complimenting a woman on her looks and making other statements. After this person's years of service, he didn't want to suffer the same fate.[8]

I told him it was a good idea to keep his mouth shut. After teaching at Brown University and working at Brookings for many years, I was keenly aware of generational and gender-based sensitivities. At the university, the faculty received anonymous course evaluations at the end of every semester, and it was always instructive to see how young people interpreted classroom comments. Offhand political statements I and others made in class were sometimes seen as evidence of deeply rooted ideological opinions or firm judgments that differed quite substantially from what was actually intended. From my own course evaluations and those of my colleagues, I learned that college students could draw broad conclusions about professors based on rather superficial evidence. That made me wary about what I said in the classroom for fear my statements might be misinterpreted or misconstrued.

Safetyism, Wokism, and Cancel Culture

Differing generational experiences take place in various ways within organizations. For example, columnist Bari Weiss explained the generational battle unfolding within her own news organization around "safetyism." She noted that "the civil war inside the *New York Times* between the (mostly young) woke [and] the (mostly 40+) liberals is the same one raging inside other publications and companies across the country. The Old Guard lives by a set of principles we can broadly call civil libertarianism. They assumed they shared that worldview with the young people they hired who called themselves liberals and progressives. But it was an incorrect assumption. The New Guard has a different worldview, one articulated best by Jon Haidt and Greg Lukianoff. They call it 'safetyism,' in which the right of people to feel emotionally and psychologically safe trumps what were previously considered core liberal values, like free speech."[9]

Years earlier, I had been in on the ground floor of the debate over tolerance, and political correctness had been launched at Brown University in the late 1980s by an enterprising student named Jeff Shesol. He later became a speechwriter for Bill Clinton and a noted author, but at Brown, he had gained acclaim by creating a popular cartoon series featuring "Mr. PC Man," a character who bent over backward to be sensitive to disenfranchised people's concerns. Through a series of cartoons, Shesol poked fun at the prevailing liberal atmosphere at Brown and gently suggested that things might have gone too far in that direction. He later syndicated a national comic strip called "Thatch," which touched on political themes.

Yet his humorous comics did little to slow Brown's movement toward inclusivity and multiculturalism. Long before it was popular elsewhere, the university inaugurated policies featuring "trigger warnings" and "safe spaces." These were educational practices designed to warn students about controversial content and shield them from objectionable ideas. Trigger warnings let students know in advance when classroom materials might raise contentious or sensitive material and allowed students to skip those classes if they thought the sessions would provoke too much emotional stress. Safe spaces referred to meetings or groups where disenfranchised groups would be protected from the dominant white male culture and could share their experiences or express their frustrations without fear of confrontation.

New York Times columnist David Brooks condemned these kinds of perspectives when he complained about parents who sheltered their children from discomfort. Citing schools that banned dodge ball on grounds that it made young people feel bad, he intoned "it's been a disaster. This overprotective impulse doesn't shelter people from fear; it makes them unprepared to deal with the fear that inevitably comes." He called for training young people "to master hardship [and] to endure suffering" and said developing tenacity should be everyone's goal.[10]

However, I felt his critique gave short shrift to the genuine struggles of many young people. Based on my experiences at Brown, there were many Ivy League students who came from nonprivileged backgrounds and were forced by economic circumstances to work their way through college. They were not entitled brats, as conservatives loved to portray them, but hardworking and highly motivated students who went on to do amazing things. They handled adversity quite well and overcame many disadvantages in their lives.

Another aspect of current life in nonprofit organizations is the tendency of some young people to talk about being "woke," that is, having a high level of awareness about power relationships and liberal virtues. Writing in the *New York Times*, author Damon Young described woke as "to recognize and reject the damage power inflicts on the most vulnerable." Even Young, though, recognized the humor of the term. "If a stranger at a dinner party is introduced—or introduces himself—as woke, I know that I'll need some whiskey before talking to him."[11]

People argued vehemently over what wokeness entailed and how it played in middle America. For example, writer Thomas Edsall asked the provocative question "is wokeness 'kryptonite for Democrats?'" Looking at public opinion polls, he showed the country sharply divided along racial, gender, and age lines. This tended to be the case on issues such as defunding the police, transgender issues, cancel culture, and university life.[12] People had very different viewpoints depending on their personal perspectives and experiences, and Edsall worried that an undue focus on cultural issues would be political suicide for Democrats.

In the woke world, young women had special language for complaining about men. One of their favorites was "mansplaining." According to the *Oxford Dictionary*, it referred to "the explanation of something by a man, typically to a woman, in a manner regarded as condescending or patronizing."[13] This practice took place when men assumed they knew more than women, when they talked over women seeking to explain something in their own area of expertise, or when men tried to sound authoritative about topics on which they knew nothing. My first wife insightfully referred to this tendency as "male answer" syndrome where men liked to answer questions even when they didn't actually know the answer.

In a related manner, there are complaints about "cultural appropriation" by powerful individuals, which occurs when someone from the dominant culture refers to or adopts an image, experience, music, or fashion from a less powerful culture. Those from the latter grouping object to these kinds of actions because they lift the experience from the context in which it occurred and miss the discrimination, racism, or domination that generated the activity.

Over the years, conservatives and free speech advocates upped the volume about the danger of muting voices. Wichita State University Tech invited Ivanka Trump to be its graduation speaker, yet it withdrew the invitation after faculty, students, and staff complained about the administration's poor handling of the George Floyd murder. Rather than calming the national mood, President Trump had poured gasoline on that murder and angered people of many persuasions. In response, Ivanka criticized the decision and said, "Our nation's campuses should be bastions of free speech. Cancel culture and viewpoint discrimination are antithetical to academia. Listening to one another is important now more than ever!"[14]

Those arguments were in line with views expressed by other leading Republicans. At a time when universities, think tanks, and nonprofits were moving toward more inclusive workspaces and confronting social inequities, GOP leaders attacked the very premise of those efforts. J. D. Vance, who had written a best-selling book about his Appalachian background and was running as a Republican for an Ohio Senate seat, made the case very clearly. In complaining about culture wars, he blamed progressive political forces for the societal discontent. "The left isn't just criticizing our country, it's not just making us ashamed of where we come from, it's trying to take our very sense of national pride and national purpose, away from us." Continuing, he argued, "It's not about correcting systemic racism or systemic wrong. It's about making us easier to control. It's about making us ashamed of where we come from."[15]

As part of our institutional discussions, we had detailed discussions over racism, sexism, and hostile work environments. In thinking about cultural issues, my Brookings colleague Jonathan Rauch worried about the possible ramifications of cancel culture for academic freedom and free speech. Interviewed by *Reason* magazine, he expressed uncertainty about the possible repression of open inquiry and signed a letter in *Harper's* warning that "the free exchange of information and ideas, the lifeblood of a liberal society, is daily becoming more constricted."[16] He cited a Cato Institute national survey that found "62% of Americans say they have political views they're afraid to share" and "32% worry their political views could harm their employment."[17]

In another interview, he warned against the spread of emotional safetyism and the desire to protect people from ideas that make them uncomfortable. In his view, such a mentality leads to intellectual conformity and, when advanced to an extreme degree, job terminations or social shaming for the offending party. "It's about organizing or manipulating a social environment or a media environment with a goal or predictable effect of isolating, deplatforming, or intimidating an ideological opponent. It's about shaping the battlefield. It's about making an idea or a person socially radioactive," he argued.[18]

Rauch traced the rise of this viewpoint back to the early 1980s when employers and universities implemented a standard known as the "hostile workplace environment" to oversee speech as well as personal conduct. "If you have to have safe environments, then you have to proactively scrub the environment of microaggressions, offensive and bigoted statements, and anything else that might cause the environment to become unsafe. That's a doctrine, which has, even conceptually, no conceivable limits," he noted.

But others within the Brookings Institution did not agree with this perspective. They wanted to keep employees safe and avoid situations that made staff members feel uncomfortable. Understanding the sensitivities of those who came from different backgrounds was part of the institutional ethos and employees were asked to respect the Brookings commitment to the human values of inclusion and diversity, and to ensure that employees operated within a safe atmosphere.

In general, the American public sided with those who felt that "canceling" someone for something they said was reasonable. When asked by the Pew Research Center how they assessed calling people out for what they said, 58 percent believed it was holding them accountable for their actions, while only 38 percent thought it was punishing people who didn't deserve it. Republicans (56 percent), though, were nearly three times as likely to think it was unfair compared to Democrats (22 percent).[19]

Yet that issue would unfold provocatively on various kinds of subjects. Variations on the themes of how people should deal with one another, what procedural and substantive rights individuals with alternative perspectives had, and how much protection Brookings should offer would sprout in many ways. It would challenge our ability to bring people together, confront external forces, and define principles and priorities.

Microbehaviors

With all the attention being paid to workplace dynamics, Brookings instituted "microbehaviors" training for scholars and staff members. The goal was to sensitize employees to the myriad ways that personal interactions could be seen negatively by other individuals. This included things such as mispronouncing names, interrupting others, rolling your eyes when other people speak, inequitable power dynamics, preferential treatment for individuals you like, understanding race and class differences, and not paying attention to less powerful staff members.

Some writers were not persuaded that these were useful programs. For example, David Brooks of the *New York Times* wrote a column ridiculing these training programs. He argued they didn't change behavior but rather reinforced existing stereotypes, failed to reduce discrimination, made white employees resentful, and pressured people to "think a certain way."[20]

But there were lots of ways such behaviors were problematic. Some men loved to discuss sports even though that excluded some women from the conversation. More powerful people interrupted statements by less powerful individuals and didn't take their comments very seriously. A few liked to tell "inside jokes" that revealed their influence but did not include others in the dialogue. And there were many ways that power distorted personal relations and created unhealthy workplace dynamics. The list could go on but the common theme was needing to have a workplace that was warm and welcoming, and open to those from a variety of backgrounds.

Gender Inequities

In the 1970s, Nixon's secretary of state, Henry Kissinger, liked to joke that "power is the ultimate aphrodisiac" to explain why he was able to date beautiful Hollywood stars despite having rather pedestrian looks.[21] According to him, being powerful put him in networks of influential people and attracted those (including models and actresses) who wanted to be associated with political power.

At that time, such behavior was not at all unusual. It was common to see powerful older men accompanied by beautiful, young companions. The men typically saw this as a perk of power and a sign of their personal magnetism. If you had power, it was completely acceptable to show it off for the entire world to see.

But fifty years later, the world has changed considerably. Dating intertwined with power is now seen as a sign of abusive men misusing their privileged positions. Being in a situation of unequal influence inherently creates unsavory dynamics and puts women in settings where their consent is compromised. After all, how can there be meaningful consent when a man has nearly all the influence in a relationship?

Figuring out how to navigate gender relationships would become a big part of my administrative responsibilities. Over the years, I mediated disputes between men and women in the workplace, sought to bring people along the path to greater inclusivity, and sometimes encountered risky situations that posed considerable challenges for all involved. It would take tremendous persistence to move the Brookings Institution toward a more inclusive direction and reach fair and equitable decisions regarding contentious issues.

Recent years have seen numerous examples of men abusing their positions. Representative Anthony Weiner went to prison for sexting with an underage woman and sending her obscene pictures. Film producer Harvey Weinstein was sentenced to twenty-six years in prison for sexually assaulting young actresses. NBC's *Today* show anchor Matt Lauer lost his job over sexual attacks in the workplace. CBS News anchor Charlie Rose was fired after he propositioned a number of his female employees.

The cases illustrate the scope of the sexual violence and misconduct taking place; a number of these episodes went well beyond sexual harassment to outright assault. Lives were damaged, and those affected revealed shocking details about how their emotional well-being had been upended and their careers derailed.

The sheer volume of these abuses led to revised workplace rules in many places. Women rightfully feel aggrieved about misogynous behavior and outright assaults. They are tired of the sexual harassment that is far too prevalent. A number of studies have shown that sexual abuse is rampant in a number of workplaces. The bad behavior can range from suggestive jokes or unwanted touching to forced dating or sexual assaults. According to one survey, "60% of women say they experience 'unwanted sexual attention, sexual coercion, sexually crude conduct, or sexist comments' in the workplace."[22]

The prevalence of sexual harassment led the Brown Club of D.C. to host a forum entitled "Are Men Animals?" which delved into how "toxic masculinity" encourages misogynous behavior. The gathering reflected the common belief among a number of young, educated people that many men are not trustworthy and are capable of a broad range of poor behavior. It featured Professor Matthew Gutman of Brown's anthropology department, who had written a book with that title, and speakers from several organizations discussing efforts to address gender-based injustices.

It isn't just universities and think tanks that are concerned about toxic and abusive men. Female employees accused *Washington Post* executives of fostering a sexist atmosphere that was harmful to them. A *Huffington Post* investigation detailed how male reporters at that news site getting death threats were receiving around-the-clock security details for seventy-two hours, whereas female reporters in a similar situation were told to go to a hotel by themselves.

At a *Washington Post* town hall in 2021, editors noted their efforts to protect reporter Seung Min Kim from anti-Asian trolling when she was covering a Biden cabinet nomination. But during that conversation, fellow writer Felicia Sonmez complained, "I wish editors had publicly supported me in the same way."[23] She had garnered a suspension for tweets about National Basketball Association star Kobe Bryant following his 2020 death in a helicopter accident. Reminding readers that Bryant had been accused of a 2003 rape, she publicized a Daily Beast article documenting the allegations about him.[24]

Although everything she tweeted about him was factually accurate, the newspaper suspended her for what it said were "ill-timed" tweets, and for a period of time, she was prohibited from covering any story that focused on sexual harassment or misconduct. Given the number of stories involving those issues, she considered the ban a major barrier to her journalistic career, although eventually the *Post* lifted its prohibition.[25] Later, Sonmez filed a lawsuit against the paper and its top editors for the ban.[26]

In addition, there were complaints at the newspaper about pay inequity and difficulties for women in winning promotions. "The place is run by men and it creates a particular atmosphere and assigns a higher value to certain male characteristics," said a female reporter. "I've been a victim of it in a broad way, as most women in the newsroom have." Another source argued, "There's a dweeby beta-male quotient at the *Post*. They're not openly macho. There's an understated respectability that is secretly pernicious and sexist operating in that place."[27]

Such complaints were common at many other organizations as well. Issues of salary inequities and unfair treatment are pervasive. According to national surveys, women make around 82 percent what men do for comparable jobs.[28] This gap has persisted for decades, despite legislation that has sought to reduce this disparity. Inequitable pay and promotions were common problems and created work conditions that were clearly unfair.

Brookings sought to take these problems seriously but was not always successful. For example, Senior Fellow Fiona Hill, who gained fame for her congressional testimony over Trump's Ukraine actions, complained about pay discrimination and sexism at the think tank. In her book, *There Is Nothing for You Here*, she noted various ways in which Brookings paid women less than deserved and excluded them from important professional networking opportunities.[29] She estimated that she had lost $500,000 of warranted pay during the course of her life.[30]

Some women feel male-run organizations don't take their complaints seriously. When female journalists, for example, get trolled on social media, which is a regular occurrence, they say male editors and executives do little to help them. "Even the most open-minded media organizations are still run by men who don't fundamentally understand the misogynistic nature of these attacks," noted one reporter.[31]

This individual's point is well-taken because most business firms are still run by men. A recent research study found that only 7 percent of Fortune 500 companies have female chief executive officers. And less than 1 percent of these firms were led by women of color.[32] Inequity was persistent and pervasive in major businesses, and women and people of color were upset regarding the lack of meaningful opportunities.

Think tanks suffered from similar problems. When I arrived at Brookings in 2008, many of its leaders were white men. It was a place that critics loved to joke was "stale, pale, and male." Long after universities had begun to diversify their top ranks, neither our trustees nor our administrators were representative of the country's demographics. Most of the board committees were chaired by men, and the board as a whole was led by them.

It took some time, but eventually things began to change. After a decade there, four of the five research vice presidents were female and/or nonwhite. The board leadership was diversified, and a number of female and minority trustees had been added.

To stay on track in this crucial area, Brookings started publishing diversity numbers on its website. People within and outside the organization could look at the gender and racial breakdowns for various groups within Brookings and see how the number varied by staff, scholars, administrators, and trustees as well as see the overtime comparisons.

We sought to make progress in the diversity of our public events. For years, many of our panels featured all white, male speakers, a practice that came to be known derisively as "manels." At a time when many of the scholars were men, all-male panels were common and a source of aggravation for those who wanted gender equity. After discussion of this issue, our program committed to getting rid of manels and making sure that gender and racial diversity prevailed at our public forums and events.

Yet even this commitment proved contentious. One day, we announced a forum with an African American female moderator and a panel of men and got lambasted online for relegating the person of color to the moderator role. Elisa Camahort Page of OpEdPagePodcast tweeted, "I AM INFURIATED. I just got an event email from @BrookingsInst to discuss hate/harassment in online gaming & how it relates to civic life WITH AN ALL-MALE PANEL (Female moderator natch). I sent an irate email (and I was so angry I cc'ed Gina from @GenderAvenger)." Continuing, she called us clueless and said that this "was a red flag for everything this country's going thru now. . . . I am unsubbing at this pt bec this makes me so angry it destroys much of the respect I had for your org."

That tweet to her 15,200 followers generated angry complaints about Brookings' chauvinism. Laura Mignott jumped in by saying, "They simply don't care and it's pathetic." Someone named Sarah chimed in, "THE BLINDNESS. If I didn't laugh, I'd cry." We added another person of color to the speaker lineup, but that did not quell the online controversy.

Furthermore, there were problems in terms of day-to-day working conditions. The maternity/paternity leave policy at Brookings was inadequate and required women to cobble together leave time, sick pay, and sometimes leaves without pay to get the time they needed following childbirth. I heard many complaints about that issue. Child care was a problem for many families as the U.S. government had minimal policies in place in terms of paid family or medical leave. That created hardship for those having to care for babies, young children, or aging relatives. This issue was a continuing source of discontent, and it was frustrating not to show faster progress.

Sometimes, the tensions arose from very down-to-earth considerations. For example, our program had gender issues in terms of bathroom access. Years earlier, the bathrooms in our program had been constructed with two urinals and two stalls in the men's room, but only one stall in the women's restroom. At that time, there were few women in the program so the configuration wasn't wildly out of whack with the numeric breakdowns in the program.

However, during the last decade, we had hired many female scholars and staff members and had reached a point where nearly two-thirds of the people on our floor were female. Having just one stall for a large number of women while there were four stalls and urinals for a much smaller number of men was clearly unfair. But our Facilities Management team came up with a creative solution to this inequity. It switched the two bathrooms, built a stall in the newly constituted women's restroom (for a total of three), and added a urinal to the new men's bathroom (for a total of two options). The transition went well, and the renovation represented one small step toward gender equity within our program.

Misconduct

Along with many other organizations, Brookings was not immune to allegations of personal misconduct. One scholar was accused of inappropriate behavior at his previous employer and was let go when Brookings learned of it. That individual later complained in a magazine profile about the way he was dealt with. Speaking to Air Mail, Leon Wieseltier criticized "the Robespierrian haste with which people's heads were chopped off before they could say a word." Continuing, he bemoaned "the fact that an allegation was tantamount to a conviction. The fact that all infractions were treated equally—there was no sense of proportion or sense of measure. And that we developed a culture of unforgivingness."[33]

His case demonstrates the challenge of delivering justice to those with complaints while also protecting the procedural rights of the accused. As a program administrator, I could be sued by either side of a workplace dispute over how I handled the complaint. If I didn't take an allegation seriously, I could be reprimanded, suspended, or terminated, and if I didn't respect the rights of the individual being investigated, that person could come after me legally for a lack of procedural due process. Any complaint was fraught with career risk, even if I had nothing to do with the original misdeed.

At Brown University, I had seen early signs of this issue in 1990 when female students, upset with the administration's failure to take sexual assault seriously, moved forcefully in this area.[34] A small group of women formed an organization called Brown Against Sexual Assault and Harassment and argued that it was time for the university to adopt stronger rules. Taking matters into their own hands, they compiled lists of "rapists, sexual assaulters, or harassers" and wrote them on bathroom walls around campus."[35]

As a result of this high-visibility protest, Brown toughened its disciplinary procedures and penalties for sexual infractions. For the first time, sexual assault was listed in the university's student conduct code as a specific offense. Those accused would face a disciplinary board of students and faculty, which could suspend or expel guilty pupils. Those who alleged sexual assault would be referred to "advocates" who would counsel them and provide procedural advice regarding how to bring charges through the disciplinary process.

But the new code did not end the controversy surrounding date rape and sexual assault. Rather, it shifted the substantive conflict to debates over procedures, rules of evidence, and the role of legal representation. There would be many disciplinary cases that would engulf the campus and generate heated debates over fairness, equity, and justice. Questions regarding whether parties to the dispute were allowed to have legal representation would rage as individual cases were adjudicated within the university's internal disciplinary process. People would lose jobs, there would be allegations of administrative malfeasance, and compromising details would be leaked to the press.

Between Brown and Brookings, I learned that virtually any contentious issue associated with an elite institution would generate negative publicity and damage the reputations of those involved. Few reporters could resist the allure of anything that sounded untoward or scandalous at a prominent organization. Those articles almost always ended up on the front page and were widely read.

Racial Injustice

Race is a crucial issue from virtually any vantage point. From the importation of slaves 400 years ago and the three-fifth's compromise in the U.S. Constitution to the Civil War and contemporary injustices regarding racial disparities in health care, wealth, educational opportunity, housing, and law enforcement, it remains one of those areas where white Americans know there are serious problems but haven't done nearly enough to address them.[36]

Every time some steps forward are made in national policy over the last few decades, there is an almost immediate backlash among white voters that slows or reverses those gains. Whites can cite many reasons not to do the right thing, and it usually takes herculean efforts to make even small progress on racial inclusion and diversity. People develop very elaborate reasons as to why certain individuals should not be hired or particular activities undertaken.

It didn't help that our internal discussions about inclusion and diversity were taking place at a time when the national political climate about race was quite poisonous. When he was in office, former president Trump openly appealed to white racists and promised them tough law enforcement and federal policies that would make America great again. To many, that sounded like making America white again, as it mostly had been in the 1950s and early 1960s before demographic change shifted the composition of the U.S. population.

In this tense U.S. situation, it was important to reconcile our institution's desire for inclusion with the national threat that white supremacists and domestic terrorists could overrun the capitol city at any given moment. I would attend our periodic seminars on racial bias, racial disparities, and microaggressions and then see armed white men encircling state and federal buildings on television. They were committing macroaggressions at the very time we were debating the nuances of microaggressions.

In speaking with minority colleagues, I learned how different their life experiences had been from mine. Although I grew up poor, I never faced racial prejudice or discrimination. I had opportunities that propelled my professional career and gave me a chance to advance socially and economically. The stories I heard were shocking. One individual said he had been stopped by the police more than two dozen times over the course of the last couple of decades for no obvious reason other than his race. Others mentioned schoolyard experiences where their classmates openly directed racial or ethnic epithets toward them.

When I was growing up, there was a popular ditty that said "sticks and stones may break my bones but words will never hurt me." The idea was that actions spoke louder than words, and people should not be sensitive about the spoken language. Yet today, it is clear that words can hurt. They can upset people and make them feel uncomfortable about their colleagues or other individuals in general.

Cognizant of this reality, I tried to be careful in describing race-related developments. During the COVID-19 pandemic, I wrote a Brookings blog post about getting the vaccination once D.C. started to inoculate those sixty-five years or older. The shot put me among the first 3 percent of Americans to receive the vaccination and provided me with a vantage point from which to observe the distribution process.[37]

On the appointed day, I showed up at the designated place and stood in line. While there, someone caught me off-guard by saying, "You don't look 65." Stunned, I turned around to defend myself only to see the person was an old friend from Brown. I hadn't seen him for a while and didn't immediately recognize him behind the mask. We stood in line for what turned out to be an hour and forty-five minutes to get the shot.

We caught up on things and then he made an astute observation. There is a problem with the vaccine distribution, he pointed out, because look who is in line. I turned around and quickly saw what he meant. Although D.C. has a population that is 62 percent minority and we were in a store located in a predominantly African American neighborhood, of the fifty people in line, nearly everyone was white. During the two hours I was there, I saw only one African American waiting to be vaccinated, and there were no Latinos or Asian Americans. It is shocking that only 2 percent of those lined up for the inoculation were minority and clearly not a good harbinger in terms of closing the racial disparity gap that has persisted throughout the pandemic.[38]

In my post, I noted these inequities and argued the clear racial disparities meant that cities and states needed to prioritize vaccines for communities that have experienced the highest COVID-19 incidence rates and had the highest financial needs. Local distributors need to recognize the reality of disparate impact by race and ethnicity, and set up community centers, outreach efforts, trusted influencers, and public education campaigns targeting those areas. Otherwise, people in those areas are going to continue to be devastated by the pandemic and suffer even more hospitalizations and fatalities.

As soon as the piece appeared, though, there were whispers about "white privilege" and an old white man getting to the head of the line, even though I had not jumped the line and did not register for the vaccination until the city started to inoculate senior citizens. I joked to friends it was the first time I appreciated being over sixty-five. But some people's reaction to the blog post showed the sensitivities that undergirded the pandemic. There were clear racial inequities in COVID-related health care, and I understood why others were upset at the pandemic's blatant inequality.

On another occasion, I had a more humorous community encounter regarding race. I went to a local barbershop after I first arrived in D.C. and asked for a haircut. The African American barber took a look at me and said, "Normally, I don't do Caucasians, I just do brothers." But he pointed to pictures on the wall featuring Black men with buzz cuts and said if I wanted something like that, he could do it. Surveying the scene, I quickly replied that was not what I was looking for and left the premises. That was one case where our differing expectations were easy to resolve.

Critical Race Theory

As a sign of the contentiousness surrounding race, conservative GOP lawmakers in 2021 launched an all-out attack on "critical race theory," a perspective designed to shed light on the long-term structural racism that has characterized U.S. policies and practices toward African Americans. Instruction about America's racist past was becoming more prevalent in U.S. schools and universities in light of the Black Lives Matter movement and the murder of innocent Black people by law enforcement. Each of those developments had fueled Black rage against racial injustice and generated a desire for stronger action and better understanding of our country's history.

Yet, as often happens in the United States, major movements toward greater justice created a backlash against possible progress. Rather than affirming the need for a full accounting about race, conservative politicians took advantage of public divisions regarding race to play to racial resentment among whites. They argued that critical stances were going too far and talking too much about "white supremacy."

Fox News helped spread this narrative as it gave the critical race theory topic widespread publicity. An analysis of its coverage in recent years showed a dramatic increase in attention in this area. Whereas the network devoted zero mentions to the topic in 2018 and four in 2019, its number of stories rose to 77 in 2020 and 626 in the first five months of 2021.[39]

In order to capitalize on concern over this movement, Republican legislators in a number of states introduced bills that banned or restricted the teaching of critical race theory in public educational institutions. Some of these bills enacted in Idaho, Iowa, Oklahoma, Tennessee, and elsewhere explicitly banned instruction of the *New York Times*'s 1619 Project that had taken a critical stance on slavery in America or other courses or programs that focused on social justice. In other places, such as Florida, state school boards banned the teaching of racial injustice themes in public schools.[40]

Such actions eliminated public funding for educational initiatives that focused on critical race theory, banned specific courses, and created possible penalties for teachers and professors who engaged in such instruction. Violation of key provisions could result in the loss of funding, job suspensions, or fines for affected professors and schools.

The passage of these restrictions was just the latest salvo in the culture wars surrounding race. Republicans sought political advan-

tage on this divisive subject by playing to the fears of their base regarding demographic change in America.[41] Whites were projected
to be in the minority by around 2044, and it was easy to stoke fears
about what that would mean for governance and public policy.

Public opinion polls showed that these attacks resonated with
the GOP base. For example, a national survey by Politico/Morning
Consult found that "54% of Republicans think critical race theory
negatively affects society, vs. 13% of Democrats." In addition, 63%
of Republicans indicated that they did not want critical race perspectives taught in K–12 schools.[42]

The GOP's tough stance on those who taught social justice and
racial inclusion meant that teachers could be subject to considerable
risk to their professions and livelihoods. Despite the principle of academic freedom that had long allowed professors to teach subjects
and perspectives based on their own professional judgment, state
legislators and policymakers were intervening directly in the classroom and limiting pedagogic prerogatives that had been mainstays
of American education.[43]

This and other steps demonstrate what a dangerous time it is for
educators. Rather than allowing educators to have autonomy and
be free of political interference, legislators were directly placing restrictions on what could be said and taught within the classroom. In
the same way think tanks and nonprofits were being delegitimized,
K–12 schools and universities were being undermined through
conservative claims of overly liberal professors holding extreme
viewpoints.

The development is an ominous sign of the power politics grip-
ping America. If you have political clout, you can simply tell others
what they can teach. You no longer have to negotiate with opponents
or tolerate people with differing points of view. You simply tell them
what they can say and how they should handle sensitive topics of
American history in school. If they don't like it, you can punish them
or force them to leave the classroom.

The backlash against the teaching of critical race theory allowed ultranationalists and outright racists to control public discourse and use the power of government to dictate their own stance on American history to everyone else. The blatant power play does not bode well for our country's ability to handle racial divisions or shift peacefully toward a multiracial and multiethnic society.

10

Survival Lessons

After more than a decade in Washington, D.C., I learned to be extremely careful in what I said and did. People can leak information about you, there can be inadvertent fallout from volatile issues, and reporters can cast you in a critical light through unflattering stories. Tweets can troll you to an international audience, your emails and Zoom calls can be hacked, your geolocation data made public, and your Venmo transactions scrutinized.

More worrisome, though, are the systemic risks. There are problems for our political regime that arise from partisan news sites, weaponized lawsuits, mob violence, ultranationalism, open attacks on science, counter-majoritarianism, and the ever-growing presence of fake news, false conspiracy theories, and what euphemistically are called alternative facts.

In this tumultuous environment, it is hard to agree on basic truths and objective realities. Illiberal sentiments have permeated American society to such a point that prominent political leaders can challenge widely held consensus over climate change, vaccinations, and election fraud, and not be scorned. Their uninformed views are taken as seriously in large parts of society as those of highly acclaimed Nobel Laureates.

These are not individual-level problems but long-term, structural threats to news reporters, opinion leaders, academic experts, and people in the knowledge sector. Disagreements over fundamental issues can lead to unfavorable news coverage, public shaming over social media, government investigations, widespread societal acceptance of falsehoods, or authoritarian behavior.[1] If government actions simply revolve around the exercise of raw political power, there is little hope our governance will be fair or equitable.

During my time in the capitol city, I witnessed media hit pieces, congressional harassment, misinformation, character assassination, subpoena requests, death threats, privacy invasions, power politics, and the degradation of democratic rights. Much of this arose from our scholars' commentary on the Trump administration, but some of it came from other parts of the political spectrum, such as business interests, wealthy donors, or the ultra-Left. As someone used to the slow pace of academia, I was shocked at all the ways during a polarized era that others could limit critical voices, undermine opponents, and take out adversaries.

It is not that think tanks, universities, and nonprofits are perfect. Having worked within two elite institutions, I have witnessed the virtues and vices of each place. Every organization has its particular problems, and Brookings and Brown are no exceptions. Like many academic institutions, neither place gets things right all the time, and outside critics raise reasonable concerns about some actions.

But when controversies arose, we dealt with them seriously, took steps to safeguard our research, and worked to ensure the integrity of our reputations. We reformed our internal processes and tried to build a more inclusive organization, even in the face of national trends that are moving in the opposite direction. We tried to be thoughtful in our policy analysis at a time when nuance is no longer in vogue. We disclosed our donors during a period when people want greater transparency surrounding fundraising.

Those things alone, though, do not safeguard our future or that of the country. The worrisome developments described in this volume have the potential to subvert American democracy and pose broad-based challenges to thought leaders, social advocates, and political analysts. The undermining of expertise and reason shatters the very basis of a science-based society.

If people think these possibilities represent hyperbole, they should pay attention to what has unfolded in Hungary, Poland, Brazil, Turkey, the Philippines, and elsewhere. These nations were working democracies whose freedoms were undermined by leaders who cracked down on the opposition and eliminated a number of procedural safeguards. In some places, academics were arrested, critics singled out, organizations threatened with legal action, and reporters and thought leaders placed under an ethical cloud.[2]

Despite the seriousness of the contemporary threats, there are a number of tips for surviving this toxic, contentious, and dangerous environment. These safeguards do not guarantee survival, but they increase the odds that people, organizations, and the political system as a whole will not be victimized by shifting political circumstances or unfair reprisals. As I outline in this chapter, these defenses are especially critical to surviving D.C. conflicts during a time of widespread partisanship, extremism, and conflict. It is crucial to understand the dangers of digital communications, the risks of a polarized political system, and the ways procedural protections have crumbled in recent years.

Guard against Copycat Candidates

Trump failed in his 2020 reelection shenanigans, but he showed other aspirants how to contest future elections. You could allege ballot fraud, try to convince local election officials to throw out suspect ballots in selected precincts, and get state officials to certify your Electoral College slate as the valid electors for Congress.

Trump may or may not run again in 2024. But regardless of what he decides, copycat candidates could pursue the same strategy as during the last presidential election. Particular leaders could play to public cynicism, claim the upcoming race was stolen, allege ballot fraud in key areas, and use the ascertainment and certification parts of the Electoral College process to make sure their side wins.

Those actions would amount to a perfectly legal coup and a successful assault on American democracy. As noted by University of California at Irvine political science professor Richard Hasen, "We face a serious risk that American democracy as we know it will come to an end in 2024."[3]

The possibility of copycat coupists suggests that the problems of U.S. democracy are not limited to Trump, and go beyond him to others who feel emboldened to contest elections. We are in a "winner-take-all" era where so many spoils go to the victor in terms of controlling public policy and key appointments that there are serious temptations to do whatever it takes to win, regardless of the legal, moral, or ethical improprieties.

In order to alter these kinds of perverse incentives, it is vital to reform the Electoral Count Act of 1887 to remove vagaries and raise the threshold for questioning campaign results.[4] For example, one thing that was sought in the Trump-Biden race was to have Vice President Mike Pence allege fraud and use his own judgment to proclaim Trump the winner. President Trump worked hard to persuade Pence to do that, but historically no vice president has asserted a solo certification role for him- or herself. To make sure that doesn't happen, Congress should close that loophole and mandate that the vice president must approve the electoral slates sent by the states and approved by the House and Senate. There should not be an independent role for the vice president in the Electoral College certification process.

In addition, right now it only takes one member of the House and Senate to launch a debate on contested certification. Given the 535 people who constitute Congress, the threshold for debate should be far higher than a single representative of each chamber. Members of Congress should amend the Electoral Count Act to require majority approval of the House and Senate to launch that kind of debate. Having a one-member requirement is way too low for such an important discussion, especially during a time when democracy is at risk.

Protect Democratic Processes

The coming years will be a major test of whether American democracy holds or folds. Looking at current developments, it could go in either direction. Those who are seeking to suppress voting have already enacted dangerous restrictions in key states. Election districts are being gerrymandered in partisan directions.[5] There have been no improvements in the Electoral Count Act of 1887 that reduce its vagueness or opportunities for mischief.

As noted in previous chapters, our current system of geography-based political representation means that political minorities are able to thwart public majorities in state legislatures, the U.S. Congress, judicial proceedings, and the Electoral College. There is a major structural malady due to the prevalence and power of counter-majoritarian institutions in the United States.

Author Thomas Mann fears the worst in this situation. Interviewed in 2021 by a news reporter, he argued, "We're on a precipice. We're actually potentially so close to losing our democracy."[6] The combination of negative developments in leadership norms, public opinion, social media, and institutional arrangements puts our government at risk of becoming illiberal. And Brookings senior fellow Fiona Hill ominously predicted in regard to Trump that "if he makes a successful return to the presidency in 2024, democracy's done."[7]

The GOP remains strong politically due to the overrepresentation of rural areas in the U.S. Senate and Electoral College and the gerrymandering of legislative districts following the 2010 and 2020 censuses. If we had direct popular election of the U.S. presidency and fair legislative districting, ultranationalist politicians would not fare very well because they are not close to political majorities on most leading issues.

Yet given our current structures, they continue to do quite well at the state and national levels. Indeed, the Republican Party can gain even greater power in the future due to its ability to suppress votes and gerrymander legislative districts. With the counter-majoritarian character of crucial political institutions, the GOP can exercise tremendous power at a time of diminishing public support.

To address these issues beyond the imperfections of the Electoral Count Act, ultimately we need to get rid of the Electoral College, establish state independent redistricting commissions, eliminate or restrict the Senate filibuster because it imposes super-majority requirements, and ensure voting rights for all eligible Americans.[8] Each of those issues is vital to democratic governance and problematic in the current situation. Contemporary efforts to limit voting and make it difficult for those living in marginalized communities to cast ballots are dangerously antidemocratic and designed to rig the system in favor of the GOP.

Resolving the issue of the Electoral College should be of urgent priority because in cases of contested elections, there are a number of ways the popular will can be thwarted.[9] For example, votes can be contested in key cities or states. Or, if a state sends competing delegate slates to Congress, the national legislative branch has the authority to decide whether the Republican or Democratic delegates get certified. There are so many outmoded vote counting and certification provisions in the Electoral Count Act that it could allow malevolent leaders to rig the election in opposition to the public will. Under some interpretations of the language, state legislatures themselves could choose the electors regardless of how the popular vote in their jurisdictions turned out.[10] If that happened, it would represent a clear repudiation of fair play and just elections.

Limit Unilateral Power

Our country needs to address risks posed by unchecked presidential powers so that we don't end up in a legal coup. Right now, chief executives can issue "emergency power" declarations that enable the leader to take extraordinary, unilateral action. In most cases, there is nothing Congress or the courts can do to limit the specific activities. That kind of unbridled influence represents a serious threat to democratic checks and balances, and a way for illiberal leaders to seize control of the country.

Congress furthermore needs to tighten powers made possible by the Insurrection Act of 1807. Designed for cases of public disorder or rebellion, the legislation allows the president to deploy federal military or state National Guard troops to quell disturbances. The Act does not define "disorder" and gives chief executives broad latitude for military action within the United States. Of course, the risk is that the outbreak of public protests could provide a rationale for presidents to invoke the Insurrection Act or declare a national emergency with unlimited powers. Either of those scenarios could move the United States to an authoritarian regime and remove valued personal freedoms and liberties.

As a sign of this threat, following street violence after the George Floyd murder in 2020, President Trump threatened to invoke the Insurrection Act and take control of certain state and local jurisdictions. He asked aides to draft a declaration and seriously considered using it to put troops on the streets in Washington, D.C., to stop looting and protests. A book by *Wall Street Journal* reporter Michael Bender says, "Trump wanted to invoke the Insurrection Act and put [General Mark] Milley in charge of a scorched-earth military campaign to suppress protests that had spiraled into riots in several cities."[11] As a sign of the seriousness of the plan, some troops were actually sent to military installations right outside the capitol city, although ultimately they were not deployed on the streets.[12]

In a number of countries, though, illiberal leaders have used exactly these kinds of provisions to undertake dictatorial actions designed to quell violence and restore order. These individuals take advantage of societal protests to institute forceful tactics that they claim will stabilize disorderly situations. Major political protests have been an excuse to declare martial law, arrest opponents, and limit personal freedoms. If we do not reform our own vehicles for unilateral power, America faces the risk that current laws could be used to suppress liberty on a broad scale.

Confront Misinformation and Propaganda

Some of the most worrying hallmarks of the contemporary era are the sheer volume of misinformation and propaganda that exists, how quickly fake facts circulate via social media, and the manner in which false information is used to go after opponents and affect the overall national conversation. We like to think that we live in an advanced time period where individuals are immune to misinformation, but that is clearly not the case.[13]

There are many false materials in circulation. These can range from gossip about prominent figures to beliefs about election integrity, vaccinations, and climate change. If lies are repeated often enough, people actually come to believe them because the sheer repetition provides external validation that convinces at least some individuals about the accuracy of the information.

Equally worrisome is how digital technology broadly enables the dissemination of these kinds of falsehoods. Deep-fake videos are examples of images that are manipulated in such realistic ways that they look like someone is saying or doing something, even though the video has been manufactured. We have long had the capacity to edit pictures, but technology now allows videos to be edited, and people are often unable to distinguish fake videos from real ones.

In this situation, it is important to confront propaganda, label deceits, and attack fabrications of reality. As my Brookings colleague Jonathan Rauch has written, we live in an era where there is a "firehose of falsehood" deployed by leading politicians. They use misinformation to divide people and build their own support. Like guerillas throwing dust in the air to distract opponents, politicians use a variety of techniques to mislead, confuse, and divert people's attention. Letting blatant lies pass without correction is dangerous, he says. Instead, it is vital to "insist loudly, unwaveringly and bravely on calling out lies."[14] Failing to do so risks personal reputations, institutional integrity, and the very essence of democracy.

But this is not just an issue of personal behavior; it is a question of public policy. We need to reform social media platforms and reduce the tendency of outlets to disseminate information in ways that fuel falsehoods, polarization, and extremism. This means enabling greater accountability on the part of large firms and making sure they uphold policies to prohibit actions that incite violence or hatred.

A Harvard University report by Tom Wheeler, Phil Verveer, and Gene Kimmelman proposes the creation of a Digital Regulatory Agency to oversee online firms.[15] With problems in terms of hate speech, misinformation, content moderation, antitrust activities, and competition policy, these authors argue it is time to create a new agency with power to require better behavior and ensure that large platforms do not enable illicit actions.

Fixing the information and communications sector would help lower the societal temperature and encourage more constructive dialogue in civil society. Democracies require respect for basic norms and laws, and until the current information ecosystem improves, our political system will remain at considerable risk.

Address Racial and Gender Inequities

Race is a tinderbox that threatens to explode at any time. Racial and gender inequities persist despite decades of people talking about the need to make progress. In spite of legislative advances in civil rights and voting rights fifty years ago, the United States now is regressing. Conservatives are playing to racist fears and stoking white resentment as they use "dog whistles" and overt racism to reach their supporters.

As an illustration of the depth of racial problems, there are dramatic wealth inequities between whites and African Americans. According to Brookings scholars Rashawn Ray and Andre Perry, "The average white family has roughly 10 times the amount of wealth as the average Black family," and this gap has worsened over the past few decades.[16] There are many reasons underlying this disparity, but systemic racism and past policy choices are major reasons for this inequality.

Figuring out how to deal with this and other issues associated with racial injustice is a vital part of the challenge facing America. Since these matters have been so intractable over such a long period of time, it will require decisive leadership, determined action, and creative thinking to address the centuries of unfairness. It is impossible to imagine the country being able to move forward without concrete progress in this area.

Political polarization makes it very difficult to address long-term racism and inequality. Leaders need to take meaningful steps to address and improve economic opportunity, provide equitable voting rights, and reduce racial disparities in health care, education, and housing. Failure to do these things will ensure that inequities persist and structural problems worsen. It will fuel racial unrest and make it impossible to move into a multiracial future.

America also needs to make progress on gender inequalities. Women face personal and professional barriers that limit their opportunities and raise their stress levels. This has been especially the case during COVID-19 as many females were forced to cope with the cumulative demands of caregiving and work. The pandemic exposed systemic flaws that have existed for a long time, but made them clearly visible for all to see. It is crucial to move forward on pay equity, economic opportunity, child care, family assistance, and political representation in order to ensure a system that is fair and equitable for all.

Be Careful about Digital Fingerprints

Forgetting about digital fingerprints is one of the most hazardous parts of D.C. life. Virtually everything that people do today leaves a digital trail. This is true for the calls people make, the texts and emails they send, the websites they visit, the geolocation data saved by their digital devices, their spending choices, and their social media commentary. Most communications today are archived and can be accessed during investigations. As many individuals have neglected to understand, there is little privacy in the digital world.[17] Law enforcement agents or government agencies can request your confidential information, and most of the time, technology firms turn over that information without much pushback on whether the material is truly relevant.

Congressman Matt Gaetz forgot this lesson when he was accused of paying female escorts. Going on Tucker Carlson's Fox News show, he vehemently denied "cash for sex" and accused his critics of a partisan witch hunt. Days later, though, reporters unearthed Venmo payments totaling $900 that he sent to his friend Joel Greenberg, who then forwarded that same amount of money to women who said they had sex with Gaetz.[18] Upon investigation, it was further alleged that Greenberg made over "150 Venmo payments to dozens of young women, and to a girl who was 17 at the time," which led to his indictment and plea bargain on trafficking charges.[19]

President Biden also fell victim to media sleuthing of his Venmo account, although in more benign ways. In 2021, BuzzFeed unearthed the chief executive's private account and easily gained access to the list of user names showing the friends and family members to whom he had transferred money over the years. There was nothing untoward in what he had done, yet the episode demonstrated the loss of privacy for prominent people living in the digital era. If Biden had not made his financial transactions private, outsiders quickly could have viewed that information and publicized it to the entire world.[20]

Law firms and private investigators hire hosts of employees and contractors who specialize in e-discovery, that is, the analysis of people's digital lives. They mine emails, texts, calls, and online activities for embarrassing statements, unethical behavior, or illegal actions. Once they have digital records, they can undertake searches for incriminating evidence. This may involve electronic searches for suspicious keywords. Depending on the suspected offense, investigators will home in on words that suggest personal malfeasance or unethical behavior.[21]

In contemporary life, the risks are greater than most people realize. One person I know said she wasn't worried about online monitoring of her work activities because she wasn't doing anything illegal. But what she didn't understand is that nonprofit organizations today have a long set of rules that go beyond law-breaking to infractions that can result in terminations, pay cuts, or demotions, even if there is no illegal behavior.

As an illustration, most organizations have rules specifying that people should not engage in actions that violate conflict of interest provisions or harm institutional reputations. The former rules are clear because people have to disclose outside speaking income greater than a certain amount and travel reimbursements from outside organizations. Those are concrete and specific criteria that are easily communicated and understood.

But what are actions that harm an organization's reputation? That is a very broad and vague standard in today's climate because there are many activities that could create reputational risk, from a poorly worded tweet to a random comment about a colleague to a research paper funded by a corporation to a speech to a foreign entity. Think tanks and universities raise millions each year from individuals, corporations, and foundations, and any paper, forum, comment, tweet, or trip can be seen externally as tainted by funding. That kind of broad reputational rule does not provide a clear standard of what people should or should not do and therefore would likely be hard to enforce in any kind of legal proceedings.

Yet that and many other organizational provisions hang over the head of every employee like the sword of Damocles. According to the Sicilian legend first told by Cicero, Damocles was a courtier to Dionysius II in the fourth century B.C. One day, the staff member told the king he was blessed to have so much power, and Dionysius offered to trade places for one day so that the courtier could experience what it was truly like to be a monarch. The individuals made the switch, but Dionysius placed a sword over the head of the temporary ruler, held in place by just a single hair, so the staffer could see the risks that accompanied extensive power.[22]

This story is appropriate for modern life because the lesson shows how in an era of corporatization, the rules have tilted in favor of employers over employees. Most private organizations today have wide latitude to discipline, suspend, or fire workers, and that creates tremendous flexibility in the administration of justice. This is particularly the case now when there are so many conservative judges appointed by elected officials who are pro-corporation. Nearly every firm has detailed rules that are administered internally by company executives with little external recourse for the employee. In some places, binding arbitration eliminates the option of external litigation. And many workers who reach a courtroom are likely to find themselves before unsympathetic judges.

At the same time, many companies have the legal ability to use keylogger software on business computers, deploy video surveillance cameras, track physical movements through geolocation software, and compile lists of visited websites and applications. They can monitor emails, social media posts, and collaboration tools and compile productivity data on how workers are spending their time. Taken together, organizations have a wide range of tools at their disposal to keep track of worker activities and penalize them for a range of different activities. There is no level playing field in corporate life, which poses considerable risks to unsuspecting employees.[23]

Use Only Oral Exchanges

There are personal risks for people operating in a highly polarized environment, and individuals need to take protective actions to safeguard their jobs and livelihoods. Not long after I started at Brookings, its then president Strobe Talbott said he needed to have an "OO" conversation with me. I had never heard that expression before so I asked him what he meant. Strobe had spent considerable time in the U.S. State Department and understood the risks of putting things in writing. He told me that "OO" meant an "only oral" exchange, which dealt with something so sensitive that he did not want to put it in an email and leave an electronic record of what had been discussed. A close friend of many prominent individuals, he had seen a number whose lives had been upended by lawsuits, e-discovery, and freedom of information requests. He did not want his communications subject to those risks so we frequently discussed sensitive topics only in person.

At first, I did not understand the virtues of this approach, but the longer I stayed in D.C. the more obvious it became that this was a valuable personal survival strategy. Not putting things in writing helped to decrease personal risk, lengthen people's careers, and safeguard organizations. During illiberal times, it is a way to guard against unfair prosecutions because information can always be used against you and, at some point in your life, probably will be used against you when you end up on the wrong side of powerful opponents.

Washington is a polarized place where alliances shift quickly as new people come into power or someone's economic or political self-interest shifts. One of famed philosopher Niccolo Machiavelli's most prominent quotes was "provinces that are easily taken are easily lost."[24] The saying by the Italian thinker basically meant that those who switch their loyalty to you can just as easily shift the other way.

The challenge today is both personal and political. People and countries that have been friendly over a period of years may shift in a direction that engenders tensions or outright hostilities. That is the case in terms of U.S. relations with several different countries and treaty obligations or trade agreements signed in the past that do not guarantee friendly future relations. People whom you count on to help you can disappear at the first sign of trouble. With all the global and domestic alterations taking place in communications, politics, and social relations, it is hard to maintain stable political alignments and personal security. Things that seem perfectly calm and predictable at one point in time can turn quickly and put you in a bad situation.

Learn from the Frontlines

The Department of Homeland Security was famous in the period following the September 11, 2001, terrorist attacks for its motto, "see something, say something."[25] It was an important reminder that everyone had valuable intelligence to offer because something that might not be apparent to organizational leaders is sometimes visible to those operating on the ground floor. Sometimes, the most relevant tips come from ordinary people who spot something atypical or out of the ordinary, such as a car parked in an unusual spot, that might represent a danger or an individual acting in a strange manner.

It is important to remember in modern life that not everything is dictated by formal structures. Every organization has informal networks where people trade information and stay abreast of new developments. Those networks rarely follow official reporting lines. Sometimes, assistant directors know more than their own directors. Or there may be staff members who work across division lines and therefore can be a valuable source of information. They regularly chat with individuals outside their own program and acquire lots of intelligence about what is happening and how people are responding to official missives. It is vital to stay in touch with those individuals because they generally know more than the official channels and therefore represent valuable sources of information.

Those at the top of the organizational pyramid should not delude themselves into thinking they have all the information within the operation. In leadership positions, it is easy to become overconfident or think you know everything. You have a high-level title, which can blind you to what is happening elsewhere around you. Wearing blinders is the worst thing leaders can do within their organizations.

One Brookings person told me he had an informal rule of meeting only with people one title above or below him. By that, he meant that he did not waste time meeting with entry-level workers in his program. He mainly wanted to deal with his organizational peers who shared his status within the institution.

However, I couldn't think of a worse way to run an operation. Spending all your time with peers is a surefire way to grow out of touch and not understand what is happening at every level within the organization. Oftentimes, my most valuable intelligence comes from research or staff assistants because they are on the frontlines and see a variety of things that can inform my decisions. For me, they represent an early warning system of issues that could become problematic down the road.

Continuing to be inquisitive is one of the most important leadership qualities in a rapidly changing environment. You should never assume you know everything that is going on around you. If you don't regularly ask questions and engage with other people, you will never survive major threats, contentious conflicts, or democracy-backsliding.

Acknowledgments

This book draws on my experiences and impressions over the last few decades. I use observations, notes, news articles, and social media posts to back up my memories. I recognize that others may have recollections that vary from mine or may draw different conclusions than I have. But I present my reminiscences based on how I recall things having taken place. Some portions of this manuscript are drawn from my earlier publications.

I wish to thank several people for their help with this book. I am indebted to Karin Rosnizeck for conversations about the work. She is a keen sounding board whose insights improved the narrative. I also want to thank John Allen for his support of this book project and conversations regarding the future of American democracy. Thanks to Norman Eisen, Elaine Kamarck, Jon Rauch, Ben Wittes, and the anonymous reviewers of this manuscript for their helpful comments and suggestions. Aminah Taariq-Sidibe provided valuable research assistance and I am very grateful for her help.

A number of individuals at the Brookings Institution Press deserve a special thank you. As they have done for many years, press director William Finan and assistant director and sales manager Yelba Quinn provided invaluable counsel. I appreciate all they have done to make the press a valuable publication outlet and an integral part of the national conversation. Cecilia González does a master job of making sure the publication trains run on time. She has provided tremendous help on many book projects and deserves a big thank you. Diane Ersepke did an outstanding job of copyediting the book, and I appreciate her thorough and detailed reading of the manuscript. None of these individuals are responsible for the interpretations in this volume.

Notes

Chapter 1

1. Part of this is drawn from John R. Allen and Darrell M. West, "Ways to Reconcile and Heal America," Brookings Institution report, February 8, 2021.

2. Darrell M. West, *Divided Politics, Divided Nation: Hyperconflict in the Trump Era* (Brookings Institution Press, 2019).

3. Steven Webster, *American Rage: How Anger Shapes Our Politics* (Cambridge University Press, 2020).

4. Katie Benner, "Trump Pressured Justice Department to Claim Election Was Corrupt," *New York Times*, July 31, 2021, p. A1.

5. Robert Kaplan, "Our Constitutional Crisis Is Already Here," *Washington Post*, September 23, 2021. See also Max Boot, "The Republican Plot to Steal the 2024 Election," *Washington Post*, June 1, 2021.

6. Thomas E. Mann and Norman J. Ornstein, *It's Even Worse Than It Looks: How the American Constitutional System Collided with the New Politics of Extremism* (New York: Basic Books, 2012).

7. Ben Sasse, *Them: Why We Hate Each Other—and How to Heal* (New York: St. Martin's, 2019).

8. Benjamin Page and Martin Gilens, *Democracy in America? What Has Gone Wrong and What We Can Do about It* (University of Chicago Press, 2020).

9. Anne Applebaum, *Twilight of Democracy: The Seductive Lure of Authoritarianism* (New York: Doubleday, 2020).

10. Thomas Edsall, "How Much Does How Much We Hate Each Other Matter?" *New York Times*, September 29, 2021.

11. Darrell M. West, *The Future of Work: Robots, AI, and Automation* (Brookings Institution Press, 2018), pp. 139–140.

12. Darrell M. West, *Divided Politics, Divided Nation: Hyperconflict in the Trump Era* (Brookings Institution Press, 2019).

13. For more details, see Darrell M. West, *Divided Politics, Divided Nation: Hyperconflict in the Trump Era* (Brookings Institution Press, 2019).

14. Darrell M. West, "Letters of a College Professor," InsidePolitics.org, 2007.

Chapter 2

1. Angie Drobnic Holan and Amy Sherman, "House Democrats Press Timeline in Day 2 of Senate Impeachment Trial," PolitiFact, February 10, 2021.

2. Michael Wolff, "Donald Trump's January 6: The View from Inside the Oval Office," *New York Magazine*, July 5, 2021.

3. Wolff.

4. Katie Benner, "Meadows Pressed Justice Dept. to Investigate Election Fraud Claims," *New York Times*, June 5, 2021, and Emma Brown, Jon Swaine, Jacqueline Alemany, Josh Dawsey, and Tom Hamburger, "Election Denier Who Circulated Jan. 6 PowerPoint Says He Met with Meadows at White House," *Washington Post*, December 11, 2021.

5. Dan Mangan and Kevin Breuninger, "Mike Pence Rejects Trump's Call to Overturn Biden Election," CNBC, January 6, 2021.

6. Joshua Kaplan and Joaquin Sapien, "New Details Suggest Senior Trump Aides Knew Jan. 6 Rally Could Get Chaotic," ProPublica, June 25, 2021.

7. Alan Feuer and Frances Robles, "Proud Boys under Growing Scrutiny in Capitol Riot Investigation," *New York Times*, January 26, 2021; and Spencer Hsu, "Latest Alleged Oath Keeper Arrested in Capitol Riot Turned Over Body Armor and Firearm," *Washington Post*, July 2, 2021.

8. Melissa Quinn, Kathryn Watson, Grace Segers, and Stefan Becket, "Democrats Use New Video, Trump Tweets to Show 'Full Scope' of Capital Attack at Impeachment Trial," CBS News, February 11, 2021.

9. Philip Rucker and Carol Leonnig, "The Inside Story of Trump's Defiance and Inaction on Jan. 6," *Washington Post*, July 15, 2021. See also Bob Woodward and Robert Costa, *Peril* (New York: Simon & Schuster, 2021), p. xix.

10. Juana Summers, "Congress Certifies Biden Victory," National Public Radio, January 7, 2021.

11. Felicia Sonmez, "Pelosi Introduces Legislation That Would Establish

Select Committee to Probe Jan. 6 Capitol Attack," *Washington Post*, June 28, 2021.

12. Harry Stevens, Daniela Santamarina, Kate Rabinowitz, Kevin Uhrmacher, and John Muyskens, "How Members of Congress Voted on Counting the Electoral College Vote," *Washington Post*, January 7, 2021.

13. Steven Levitsky and Daniel Ziblatt, *How Democracies Die* (New York: Crown, 2019).

14. Norman Eisen, Joshua Matz, Donald Ayer, Gwen Keyes Fleming, Colby Galliher, Jason Harrow, and Raymond Tolentino, *Fulton County, Georgia's Trump Investigation*, Brookings Institution Report, October 4, 2021.

15. Cortney Moore, "What Is the Insurrection Act?" Fox Business, June 1, 2020; and Christine Hauser, "What Is the Insurrection Act of 1807?" *New York Times*, June 2, 2020.

16. Elizabeth Goitein, "The Alarming Scope of the President's Emergency Powers," *The Atlantic*, January/February, 2019.

17. Goitein, "The Alarming Scope."

18. Reid Epstein, "Wisconsin Republicans Push to Take Control of State's Elections," *New York Times*, November 20, 2021, p. A10.

19. Brennan Center for Justice, "State Voting Bills Tracker, 2021," New York University, May 28, 2021; and Nick Corasaniti and Reid Epstein, "How Republican States Are Expanding Their Power over Elections," *New York Times*, June 19, 2021.

20. Richard Hasen, "Identifying and Minimizing the Risk of Election Subversion and Stolen Elections in the Contemporary United States," SSRN, September 18, 2021.

21. Michael Wines, "As Washington Stews, State Legislatures Increasingly Shape American Politics," *New York Times*, August 29, 2021.

22. Richard Hasen, "The Supreme Court Is Putting Democracy at Risk," *New York Times*, July 1, 2021, p. A19.

23. Adam Liptak, "Supreme Court Upholds Arizona Voting Restrictions," *New York Times*, July 1, 2021.

24. Michael Holt, *By One Vote* (University Press of Kansas, 2008).

25. Eric Foner, *Reconstruction: America's Unfinished Revolution, 1863–1877* (New York: Harper and Row, 1988).

26. Edward Foley, *Ballot Battles: The History of Disputed Elections in the United States* (Oxford University Press, 2016).

27. Philip Bump, "What Did John Eastman Really Want to Have Happen?" *Washington Post*, November 1, 2021.

28. University of Virginia Center for Politics newsletter, "UVA Center for

Politics and Project Home Fire Use Innovative Polling and Data Analytics to Identify America's Political Fissures and Explain Ways to Foster Compromise," Charlottesville, Virginia, October 3, 2021.

29. Thomas Edsall, "How Far Are Republicans Willing to Go? They're Already Gone," *New York Times*, June 9, 2021.

30. GoLocalProv, "Fate of Michael Flynn's Honorary Degree: Cancel Culture v. QAnon Hero," June 1, 2021.

31. Ronald Daniels, "Why Authoritarian Regimes Attack Independent Universities," *Washington Post*, September 28, 2021. Also see Ronald Daniels, *What Universities Owe Democracy* (Johns Hopkins University Press, 2021).

32. Thomas Patterson, *How America Lost Its Mind: The Assault on Reason That's Crippling Our Democracy* (University of Oklahoma Press, 2019).

33. Steven Livingston and Lance Bennett, "The Institutional Crisis at the Root of Our Political Disinformation and Division," Social Science Research Council, October 20, 2020.

34. W. Lance Bennett and Steven Livingston, eds., *The Disinformation Age: Politics, Technology, and Disruptive Communication in the United States* (Cambridge University Press, 2020).

Chapter 3

1. Darrell M. West, *Megachange: Economic Disruption, Political Upheaval, and Social Strife in the 21st Century* (Brookings Institution Press, 2016).

2. Paul Barrett, Justin Hendrix, and Grant Sims, "How Tech Platforms Fuel U.S. Political Polarization and What Government Can Do about It," Brookings Institution, *TechTank* (blog), September 27, 2021.

3. Edelman Trust Barometer, *Global Report*, January, 2020, p. 15.

4. Michael Grynbaum and Marc Tracy, "Trump Campaign Sues *New York Times* Over 2019 Opinion Article," *New York Times*, February 26, 2020.

5. Paul Farhi, "Trump Campaign Sues *Washington Post* Over Opinion Columns Asserting Link to Russian Election Interference," *Washington Post*, March 3, 2020.

6. Jonathan Stempel, "Trump Campaign Sues CNN for Libel Over Russia Opinion Piece," Reuters, March 6, 2020.

7. Erik Wemple, "Judge Tosses Absurd Trump Campaign Lawsuit against the *New York Times*," *Washington Post*, March 10, 2021.

8. Benjamin Din, "Apple's Privacy Headache," *Morning Tech* (Politico), June 14, 2021.

9. Katie Benner, Nicholas Fandos, Michael Schmidt, and Adam Goldman, "Hunting Leakers, Justice Dept. Got Democrats' Data," *New York Times*, June

11, 2021; and Nicholas Fandos and Charlie Savage, "Inquiry Opened Into Secret Push to Seize Records," *New York Times*, June 12, 2021.

10. Paul Farhi, "TV News Crews Are Increasingly Threatened with Violence on the Job," *Washington Post*, July 9, 2021.

11. Eric Kolenich, "The Republican Party of Virginia Isn't Happy with Larry Sabato's Tweets," *Richmond Times Dispatch*, July 9, 2021.

12. Michael Wines, "Florida Bars Professors from Testifying as Expert Witnesses in Voting Case," *New York Times*, October 30, 2021, p. A17, and Andrew Jeong, "University of Florida Bars Faculty Members from Testifying in Voting Rights Lawsuit against DeSantis Administration," *Washington Post*, October 30, 2021.

13. Lori Rozsa and Susan Svrluga, "Professors Sue University of Florida, Claiming Free Speech Restraints," *Washington Post*, November 5, 2021.

14. Shibley Telhami and Stella Rouse, "America First? American National Identity Declines Over Last Two Years among Both Republicans and Democrats," University of Maryland Critical Issues Poll, November 2017.

15. Jacob Hacker and Paul Pierson, *Winner-Take-All Politics: How Washington Made the Rich Richer—and Turned Its Back on the Middle Class* (New York: Simon & Schuster, 2010).

16. Larry Sabato, Kyle Kondik, and Miles Coleman, eds., *A Return to Normalcy? The 2020 Election That (Almost) Broke America* (Lanham, MD: Rowman & Littlefield, 2021); and Jonathan Rauch, *The Constitution of Knowledge: A Defense of Truth* (Brookings Institution Press, 2021).

17. Katie Hill, "It's Not Over for Me Yet," *New York Times*, December 8, 2019.

18. Isabella Paz, "Women Running for Office Have to Worry about One More Thing: Their Phones," *New York Times*, November 9, 2019.

19. Sheri Madigan et al., "Prevalence of Multiple Forms of Sexting Behavior among Youth," *Journal of the American Medical Association Pediatrics*, 172, no. 4 (February 26, 2018), 327–35.

20. Quinta Jurecic, "The Humiliation of Katie Hill Offers a Warning," *The Atlantic*, October 31, 2019.

21. Katie Hill, "It's Not Over for Me Yet," *New York Times*, December 8, 2019.

22. Jessica Bennett, "Don't Fence Her In," *New York Times*, August 9, 2020.

23. Max Fisher, "Disinformation for Hire, Shadow Industry, Is Quietly Booming," *New York Times*, July 25, 2021.

24. Aaron Krolik and Kashmir Hill, "The Slander Industry," *New York Times*, April 24, 2021.

25. Democracy Forward, "Democracy Forward Requests Information into Whether Trump DHS Officials Violated Privacy Law by Leaking Individuals' Immigration Status to Fox News, Breitbart," May 11, 2020.

26. Shawn Boburg, "Commerce Department Security Unit Evolved Into Counterintelligence-Like Operation," *Washington Post*, May 24, 2021; and Catie Edmondson, "Race Motivated Agency Spying, Report Reveals," *New York Times*, July 17, 2021.

27. Amy Burroughs, "How To Create an Equitable Digital Culture in K-12," *Ed Tech*, July 22, 2020.

28. Heather Kelly, "A Priest's Phone Location Data Outed His Private Life. It Could Happen to Anyone," *Washington Post*, July 22, 2021; and Michelle Boorstein, Marisa Iati, and Elahe Izadi, "A Catholic Newsletter Promised Investigative Journalism. Then It Outed a Priest Using Grindr Data," *Washington Post*, July 24, 2021.

29. Liam Stack, "New Catholic Controversy: Priests on Dating Apps," *New York Times*, August 22, 2021, p. 17.

30. Shoshana Zuboff, *The Age of Surveillance Capitalism: The Fight for a Human Future at the New Frontier of Power* (New York: Public Affairs, 2020).

31. Kevin Poulsen, Robert McMillan, and Dustin Volz, "SolarWinds Hack Victims: From Tech Companies to a Hospital and University," *Wall Street Journal*, December 21, 2020.

32. Ellen Nakashima, "Biden Administration Moving to Address a Global Compromise by Chinese and Other Hackers of Microsoft Email Servers," *Washington Post*, March 6, 2021.

33. Michael Shear, Nicole Perlroth, and Clifford Krauss, "Colonial Pipeline Paid Roughly $5 Million in Ransom to Hackers," *New York Times*, May 13, 2021.

34. Souad Mekhennet and Craig Timberg, "Nearly 25,000 Email Addresses and Passwords Allegedly from NIH, WHO, Gates Foundation and Others Are Dumped Online," *Washington Post*, April 22, 2020.

35. Marc Fisher, "U.N. Ties Alleged Bezos Phone Hacking to Post's Coverage of Saudi Arabia," *Washington Post*, January 22, 2020.

36. Brad Stone, "Come At Me," *Bloomberg Businessweek*, May 10, 2021.

37. Emily Flitter and James Stewart, "Bill Gates Met With Jeffrey Epstein Many Times, Despite His Past," *New York Times*, October 12, 2019; Emily Kirkpatrick, "Bill Gates's Meetings With Jeffrey Epstein Are Apparently a 'Sore Spot' for Melinda," *Vanity Fair*, May 13, 2021; Emily Glazer and Khadeeja Safdar, "Melinda Gates Was Meeting with Divorce Lawyers Since 2019 to End Marriage with Bill Gates," *Wall Street Journal*, May 9, 2021; and Timothy

Bella, "Bill Gates Says He Regrets Relationship with Jeffrey Epstein: 'It Was a Huge Mistake,'" *Washington Post*, August 5, 2021.

38. Emily Glazer, Justin Baer, Khadeeja Safdar, and Aaron Tilley, "Bill Gates Left Microsoft Board amid Probe into Prior Relationship with Staffer," *Wall Street Journal*, May 16, 2021.

39. Emily Glitter and Matthew Goldstein, "Long Before Divorce, Bill Gates Had Reputation for Questionable Behavior," *New York Times*, May 16, 2021.

40. Paul Sullivan, "If Bezos Can Get Hacked, You Can Too," *New York Times*, February 1, 2020, p. B6.

41. Fiona Hill, *There Is Nothing for You Here* (Boston: Mariner Books, 2021).

42. Christopher Keating, "Quinnipiac Poll: 77% of Republicans Believe There Was Widespread Fraud in the Presidential Election," *Hartford Courant*, December 10, 2020.

43. Karl Racine and others, "Motion for Leave to File and Brief," Supreme Court amici curiae brief number 220155, December 2020.

44. Jonathan Rauch, *The Constitution of Knowledge: A Defense of Truth* (Brookings Institution Press, 2021).

45. Aaron Blake, "Kellyanne Conway Says Donald Trump's Team Has 'Alternative Facts,'" *Washington Post*, January 22, 2017.

46. Naomi Oreskes and Erik Conway, *Merchants of Doubt: How a Handful of Scientists Obscured the Truth on Issues from Tobacco Smoke to Climate Change* (London: Bloomsbury Publishing, 2011).

47. Eric Lipton and Kenneth Vogel, "Test of Ethics Awaits Biden and His Team," *New York Times*, November 29, 2020.

48. Yeganeh Torbati and Beth Reinhard, "Neera Tanden, Biden's Pick for Budget Chief, Runs a Think Tank Backed by Corporate and Foreign Interests," *Washington Post*, December 5, 2020.

49. Aaron Blake, "So What Is the Neera Tanden Standard?" *Washington Post*, February 22, 2021.

50. Jacob Jarvis, "Neera Tanden Once Criticized Joe Manchin's Pharma CEO Daughter," *Newsweek*, February 24, 2021.

51. Jacob Hacker and Paul Pierson, *Let Them Eat Tweets: How the Right Rules in an Age of Extreme Inequality* (New York: Liveright, 2021).

52. Matthew Crawford, "How Science Has Been Corrupted," UnHerd, May 3, 2021.

Chapter 4

1. Darrell M. West, *Divided Politics, Divided Nation: Hyperconflict in the Trump Era* (Brookings Institution Press, 2019); and Jeffrey Berry and Sarah Sobieraj, *The Outrage Industry: Political Opinion Media and the New Incivility* (Oxford University Press, 2014).

2. Adam Liptak and Alicia Parlapiano, "What the Public Thinks about Major Supreme Court Cases This Term," *New York Times*, June 1, 2021.

3. Seymour Martin Lipset and William Schneider, *The Confidence Gap* (New York: Free Press, 1983).

4. Michael Dimock and Richard Wike, "America Is Exceptional in the Nature of Its Political Divide," Pew Research Center, November 13, 2020.

5. Sean Kates, Jonathan Ladd, and Joshua Tucker, "Should You Worry about American Democracy?" *Washington Post*, October 24, 2018.

6. CBS News, "Americans See Democracy under Threat," January 17, 2021.

7. Jennifer Agiesta and Ariel Edwards-Levy, "Most Americans Feel Democracy Is Under Attack in the US," CNN, September 15, 2021.

8. Public Religion Research Institute, "Competing Visions of America: An Evolving Identity or a Culture Under Attack? Findings from the 2021 American Values Survey," November 1, 2021.

9. Matthew MacWilliams, "Trump Is an Authoritarian. So Are Millions of Americans," *Politico Magazine*, September 23, 2020.

10. Cameron Easley, "U.S. Conservatives Are Uniquely Inclined toward Right-Wing Authoritarianism Compared to Western Peers," Morning Consult, June 28, 2021.

11. Darrell M. West, *Megachange: Economic Disruption, Political Upheaval, and Social Strife in the 21st Century* (Brookings Institution Press, 2016).

12. William Gale and Darrell M. West, "Is the US Headed for Another Civil War?" *FixGov* (blog), Brookings Institution, September 16, 2021.

13. Patrick Murray, "American Electorate," Monmouth University Polling Institute, August 25, 2020.

14. Patrick Murray, "Study Finds Differences between Two Types of Supporters," Monmouth University Polling Institute, January 19, 2021.

15. Sally Satel, "The Myth That Authoritarianism Happens Only on the Right," *The Atlantic*, September 25, 2021.

16. Lee Drutman, Larry Diamond, and Joe Goldman, "Follow the Leader: Exploring American Support for Democracy and Authoritarianism," Democracy Fund Voter Study Group, March 2018.

17. Robert Griffin and Mayesha Quasem, "Crisis of Confidence: How Election 2020 Was Different," Democracy Fund Voter Study Group, June 2021.

Chapter 5

1. Steven Levitsky and Daniel Ziblatt, "The Biggest Threat to Democracy Is the GOP Stealing the Next Election," *The Atlantic*, July 9, 2021.

2. Thomas Edsall, "Trump Won't Let America Go," *New York Times*, December 12, 2021.

3. Darrell M. West, "It's Time to Abolish the Electoral College," Brookings Institution, October 15, 2019.

4. Mark Muro, Eli Byerly-Duke, Yang You, and Robert Maxim, "Biden-Voting Counties Equal 70% of America's Economy," Brookings Institution Metropolitan Policy, November 10, 2020.

5. Ezra Klein, "David Shor Is Telling Democrats What They Don't Want to Hear," *New York Times*, October 8, 2021.

6. Quoted in E. J. Dionne, "The Hypocrisy Argument on the Filibuster Is Itself Phony," *Washington Post*, November 28, 2021.

7. John Johnson, "Why Do Republicans Overperform in the Wisconsin State Assembly? Partisan Gerrymandering vs. Political Geography," Marquette University Law School Blog, February 11, 2021.

8. Kyle Kondik, "Redistricting in America, Part One: Gerrymandering Potency Raises the Stakes for the 2020s," *Sabato's Crystal Ball* (newsletter), University of Virginia Center for Politics, July 22, 2021.

9. Portions of this section are drawn from Darrell M. West, *Billionaires: Reflections on the Upper Crust* (Brookings Institution Press, 2014).

10. Benjamin Page, Larry Bartels, and Jason Seawright, "Democracy and the Policy Preferences of Wealthy Americans," *Perspectives on Politics*, 11 (March 2013), 51–73.

11. Page, Bartels, and Seawright.

12. Sam Levine, "US Sinks to New Low in Rankings of World's Democracies," *The Guardian*, March 24, 2021.

Chapter 6

1. Susan Hennessey and Benjamin Wittes, *Unmaking the Presidency: Donald Trump's War on the World's Most Powerful Office* (New York: Farrar, Straus and Giroux, 2020).

2. Katie Benner, "Report Cites New Details of Trump Pressure on Justice Dept. Over Election," *New York Times*, October 6, 2021.

3. Sol Stern, "Think Tank in the Tank," *Democracy*, July 7, 2020.

4. Stern.

5. Ken Vogel, "New America, a Google-Funded Think Tank, Faces Backlash for Firing a Google Critic," *New York Times*, September 1, 2017.

6. Jennifer Shuessler, "Leader of Prestigious Yale Program Resigns, Citing Donor Pressure," *New York Times*, September 30, 2021.

7. Shuessler.

8. Jane Mayer, *Dark Money: The Hidden History of the Billionaires behind the Rise of the Radical Right* (New York: Anchor Books, 2017). See also David Wessel, *Only the Rich Can Play: How Washington Works in the New Gilded Age* (New York: PublicAffairs, 2021).

9. Darrell M. West, *Billionaires: Reflections on the Upper Crust* (Brookings Institution Press, 2014).

10. Daniel Drezner, *The Ideas Industry: How Pessimists, Partisans, and Plutocrats Are Transforming the Marketplace of Ideas* (Oxford University Press, 2017).

11. Darrell M. West, "Letters of a College Professor," InsidePolitics.org, 2007.

12. Aaron Klein, "Alleged 'WhistleBlower' Eric Ciaramella Worked Closely with Anti-Trump Dossier Hoaxer," Breitbart, November 6, 2019.

13. David Frum, "A Gangster in the White House," *The Atlantic*, December 27, 2019.

14. Sharyl Attkisson, "The Curious Timeline for Taking Trump," *The Hill*, November 8, 2019.

15. Julie Kelly, "Brookings Institution Flush with Qatari Cash, NeverTrump Donors," Center for American Greatness, July 27, 2020.

16. Julie Kelly, "Brookings Institution: A Key Collusion Collaborator," Center for American Greatness, July 23, 2020.

17. Joe Hoft, "With Huge Financial Backing from Hostile Foreign Entities Brookings Institute Is Working to Help Democrats Win in 2020," *Gateway Pundit*, July 29, 2020.

18. Asawin Suebsaeng and Adam Rawnsley, "Website Run by 'Dumbest Man on the Internet' Helped Fuel Trump's Effort to Cancel Democracy," Daily Beast, August 4, 2021.

19. Joshua Klein, "Rep. Devin Nunes: Brookings Institution Disseminated the Dossier," Breitbart, July 24, 2020.

20. Paul Sperry, "Meet the Steele Dossier's 'Primary Subsource': Fabulist Russian at Democrat Think Tank Whose Boozy Past the FBI Ignored," RealClearInvestigations, July 24, 2020.

21. Sperry.

22. Shane Harris, "DHS Compiled 'Intelligence Reports' on Journalists Who Published Leaked Documents," *Washington Post*, July 30, 2020.

23. Harris.

24. John Hudson, "Key Impeachment Witness Gordon Sondland Sues

Mike Pompeo and U.S. for $1.8 Million in Legal Fees," *Washington Post*, May 24, 2021.

25. Charlie Savage and Adam Goldman, "Subpoenaing the Brookings Institution, Durham Focuses on Trump-Russia Dossier," *New York Times*, April 12, 2021.

26. Adam Goldman and Charlie Savage, "Authorities Arrest Analyst Who Contributed to Steele Dossier," *New York Times*, November 4, 2021.

27. Margot Cleveland, "Why Special Counsel John Durham Subpoenaed the Brookings Institution," *The Federalist*, November 12, 2021.

28. Jonathan Turley, "This Liberal Think Tank Keeps Popping Up in Durham Investigation," Fox News, November 8, 2021.

29. Justin Rohrlich, "Louisiana Man Promised 'Most Heinous' Deaths for Brookings Staffers," Daily Beast, June 21, 2021.

30. Steven Teles and Jessica Gover, "The American Enterprise Institute's Near-Death Experience," Johns Hopkins University Stavros Niarchos Foundation Agora Institute, December, 2020.

31. Mike Gonzalez, "Do You Like to Be Nudged?" The Heritage Foundation, March 13, 2014.

32. Jonathan O'Connell, "Aspen Institute Think Tank Receives $8 Million Federal Small-Business Loan," *Washington Post*, May 13, 2020.

33. O'Connell.

34. Jonathan O'Connell, "Aspen Institute to Return $8 Million in Small Business Funds," *Washington Post*, May 14, 2020.

35. Daniel Lippman, "A War Over Russia Has Erupted at the Atlantic Council," Politico, March 11, 2021.

36. James McGann, "2020 Global Go To Think Tank Index Report," University of Pennsylvania, 2021, p. 350.

37. Glenn Kessler, Salvador Rizzo, and Meg Kelly, "President Trump Made 16,241 False or Misleading Claims in His First Three Years," *Washington Post*, January 20, 2020.

38. David Dayen, "Google's Guardians," *American Prospect*, October 26, 2020.

39. Darrell M. West, "Questions for Technology CEOs Testifying before Congress," Brookings *TechTank* (blog), July 14, 2020.

40. Alex Kotch, "Centrist Third Way, Funded by Corporate Interests, Attacks Sanders in Iowa," PR Watch, January 31, 2020.

41. Tom Hamburger, "How Elizabeth Warren Picked a Fight with Brookings—and Won," *Washington Post*, September 29, 2015.

42. Hamburger.

43. Craig Silverman and Ryan Mac, "New York Times Columnist David

Brooks Blogged for Facebook's Corporate Site," BuzzFeed News, February 26, 2021; and Craig Silverman and Ryan Mac, "Facebook Helped Fund David Brooks's Second Job," BuzzFeed News, March 3, 2021.

44. Paul Farhi, "David Brooks of *New York Times* Criticized for Undisclosed Financial Ties to Project He Praised," *Washington Post*, March 4, 2021.

45. Paul Farhi, "*New York Times* Columnist Resigns from Think Tank amid Conflict-of-Interest Controversy," *Washington Post*, March 6, 2021.

46. Julian Barnes and David Sanger, "Saudi Crown Prince Is Held Responsible for Khashoggi Killing in U.S. Report," *New York Times*, February 26, 2021.

47. Adam Kredo, "U.S. Think Tank Under Fire for Hosting Top Iranian Official," Washington Free Beacon, September 15, 2020.

48. Eliana Johnson, "At the Atlantic Council, Foreign Money Talks," Washington Free Beacon, August 7, 2020.

49. Kemal Kirisci, "Turkey's Downward Spiral and the Scuffles at Erdoğan's Brookings Speech," Brookings Institution, *Order From Chaos* (blog), April 4, 2016.

50. Nahal Toosi, "Trump Administration Demands Think Tanks Disclose Foreign Funding," Politico, October 13, 2020.

51. Kenneth Vogel and Benjamin Novak, "Hungary's Leader Fights Criticism in U.S. Via Vast Influence Campaign," *New York Times*, October 4, 2021.

Chapter 7

1. Marvin Kalb, *Enemy of the People: Trump's War on the Press, the New McCarthyism, and the Threat to American Democracy* (Brookings Institution Press, 2018).

2. Betsy Woodruff Swan, "Inside DOJ's Nationwide Effort to Take on China," Politico, April 7, 2020. Also see Ellen Nakashima and David Nakamura, "China Initiative Aims to Stop Economic Espionage. Is Targeting Academics Over Grant Fraud 'Overkill?'" *Washington Post*, September 15, 2021.

3. Ellen Barry, "Professor Sues Harvard after His Arrest," *New York Times*, October 10, 2020.

4. David Nakamura and Ellen Nakashima, "Mistrial in Justice Dept. Fraud Case against College Professor Prompts Renewed Scrutiny of Agency's 'China Initiative,'" *Washington Post*, June 17, 2021.

5. Jamie Horsley, "It's Time for a New Policy on Confucius Institutes," Lawfare Institute, *Lawfare* (blog), April 1, 2021.

6. Elizabeth Redden, "Closing Confucius Institutes," *Inside Higher Education*, January 9, 2019.

7. Gabe Bullard, "Following Federal Pressure, UMD Will Close a Program That Had Chinese Government Support," American University Radio, WAMU, January 17, 2020.

8. Collin Binkley, "Trump Administration Reviewing Foreign Money to US Colleges," Associated Press, June 13, 2019; and Lily Jackson, "What Is It about Confucius Institutes That Spooks Lawmakers?" *Chronicle of Higher Education*, February 28, 2019.

9. U.S. Department of Education website, "U.S. Department of Education Uncovers Vast Underreporting of Foreign Gifts and Contracts by Higher Education Institutions," October 20, 2020.

10. Catherine Dunn, "Penn Got $258 Million in Foreign Money, and There May Be More It Hadn't Disclosed," *Philadelphia Inquirer*, February 24, 2020.

11. John Pomfret, "Why Are U.S. Institutions Working with Scientists Linked to China's Military Modernization?" *Washington Post*, July 30, 2020.

12. Edward Wong, "China Threatens to Detain Americans If U.S. Prosecutes Chinese Scholars," *New York Times*, October 18, 2020.

13. Alana Goodman, "Brookings Institution Partnered with Shanghai Policy Center under Scrutiny for Spying," *Washington Free Beacon*, August 14, 2020.

14. Goodman.

15. Barry Meier, *Spooked: The Trump Dossier, Black Cube, and the Rise of Private Spies* (New York: HarperCollins, 2021).

16. Eric Lipton, Brooke Williams, and Nicholas Confessore, "Foreign Powers Buy Influence at Think Tanks," *New York Times*, September 6, 2014.

17. Susan Corke, Norman Eisen, Jonathan Katz, Andrew Kenealy, James Lamond, Alina Polyakova, and Torrey Taussig, "Democracy Playbook 2021: 10 Commitments for Advancing Democracy," Brookings Institution report, December 2021.

18. Fox News "Tucker Carlson" Segment with Darren Beattie of *Revolver*, September 15, 2020.

19. Darren Beattie, "Meet Norm Eisen: Legal Hatchet Man and Central Operative in the 'Color Revolution' against President Trump," *Revolver* comments section, September 9, 2020.

Chapter 8

1. Cristiano Lima, "Tech Think Tank Chief to Step Down after Trump Death Threat," Politico, March 13, 2020.

2. Ben Smith, "Inside the Revolts Erupting in America's Big Newsrooms," *New York Times*, June 7, 2020.

3. Ben Smith, "Marty Baron Made the *Post* Great Again. Now, the News Is Changing," *New York Times*, June 28, 2020.

4. Sheera Frenkel and Cecilia Kang, *An Ugly Truth: Facebook's Battle for Domination* (New York: Harper, 2021).

5. Anne Applebaum and Peter Pomerantsev, "How to Put Out Democracy's Dumpster Fire," *The Atlantic*, April 2021.

6. *WBUR News*, "In Our Viral World, a Closer Look at Teen's Confrontation with Native American Elder," January 22, 2019.

7. Paul Farhi, "*Washington Post* Settles Lawsuit with Family of Kentucky Teenager," *Washington Post*, July 24, 2020.

8. Michael Shear, Maggie Haberman, Nicholas Confessore, Karen Yourish, Larry Buchanan, and Keith Collins, "Office of Presidency Transformed by Force of Thousands of Tweets," *New York Times*, November 3, 2019.

9. Jonathan Chait, "The Still-Vital Case for Liberalism in a Radical Age," *National Interest*, June 11, 2020.

10. Ezra Klein, "David Shor Is Telling Democrats What They Don't Want to Hear," *New York Times*, October 8, 2021.

11. Jonathan Chait, "The Still-Vital Case for Liberalism in a Radical Age," *National Interest*, June 11, 2020.

12. Michael Powell, "How a Famous Harvard Professor Became a Target Over His Tweets," *New York Times*, July 15, 2020.

13. Women's Media Center, "Who Experiences Abuse?" undated.

14. Dan Levin, "Colleges Revoke Offers Over Slurs and Screeds," *New York Times*, July 3, 2020, p. A19.

15. Anti-Defamation League, "Online Hate and Harassment Report: The American Experience 2020," June 2020.

16. Sono Shah, Emma Remy, and Aaron Smith, "Differences in How Republicans and Democrats Behave on Twitter," Pew Research Center, October 15, 2020; and Stefan Wojcik and Adam Hughes, "Sizing Up Twitter Users," Pew Research Center, April 24, 2019.

17. Mike Allen, "Blunt 2020 Lessons for Media," *Axios AM*, November 20, 2020.

18. *Wall Street Journal* Editorial Board, "A Dangerous Pick at Justice," May 12, 2021.

19. Darrell M. West, "Letters from Washington, D.C.," unpublished, 2021.

20. Bryan Pietsch, "Devin Nunes Can't Sue Twitter Over Cow and Mom Parodies, Judge Says," *New York Times*, June 25, 2020.

21. Charlie Savage, "Trump Justice Dept. Tried to Use Grand Jury to Identify Nunes Critic on Twitter," *New York Times*, May 17, 2021.

22. Savage.

23. Asawin Suebsaeng, "Trump Wanted His Justice Department to Stop 'SNL' from Teasing Him," Daily Beast, June 22, 2021.

24. Alex Kantrowitz, "How Saudi Arabia Infiltrated Twitter," BuzzFeed News, February 19, 2020.

25. Mark Sweney, "FT Suspends Journalist Accused of Listening to Rival Outlets' Zoom Calls," *The Guardian,* April 27, 2020.

26. Jeremy Barr, "The *New Yorker* Suspends Writer Jeffrey Toobin After Accidental Zoom Exposure," *Washington Post,* October 19, 2020; and Katie Robertson, "Jeffrey Toobin Is Fired by the *New Yorker,*" *New York Times,* November 11, 2020.

27. Ben Feuerherd, "O.J. Simpson Mocks Jeffrey Toobin's Zoom Incident," Fox News, October 19, 2020.

28. Katherine Rosman and Jacob Bernstein, "The Undoing of Jeffrey Toobin," *New York Times,* December 15, 2020.

29. Jessica Grose, "Is the Group Chat Sacred?" *New York Times,* February 20, 2021.

30. Michael Paulson and Sopan Deb, "How Outrage Built Over a Shakespearean Depiction of Trump," *New York Times,* June 12, 2017.

31. Molly Worthen, "The Fight Over Tenure Is Not Really about Tenure," *New York Times,* September 20, 2021.

Chapter 9

1. Nathan Glazer and Daniel Patrick Moynihan, *Beyond the Melting Pot* (MIT Press, 1970).

2. Walter Benn Michaels, *The Trouble with Diversity: How We Learned to Love Identity and Ignore Inequality* (London: Picador, 2016).

3. Sean Illing, "Millennials Are Stuck in the World Boomers Built," Vox, March 31, 2021.

4. Jonathan Rauch, *The Constitution of Knowledge: A Defense of Truth* (Brookings Institution Press, 2021).

5. Ian Ward, "The Democrats' Privileged College-Kid Problem," Politico, October 9, 2021.

6. Gabriela Schulte, "Younger Voters More Likely to Identify as 'Liberal' on Economic and Social Issues," *The Hill,* June 10, 2020.

7. Colby Itkowitz, "The Next Generation of Voters Is More Liberal, More Inclusive, and Believes in Government," *Washington Post,* January 17, 2019.

8. Sarah Ellison and Paul Farhi, "The End of the Chris Matthews Era: How the Bombastic Host Got Forced Out at MSNBC," *Washington Post,* March 3,

2020; and Laura Bassett, "Like Warren, I Had My Own Sexist Run-In with Chris Matthews," *GQ*, February 28, 2020.

9. Bari Weiss, June 4, 2020, tweets.

10. David Brooks, "The Age of Coddling Is Over," *New York Times*, April 17, 2020, p. A27.

11. Damon Young, "In Defense of 'Woke,'" *New York Times*, December 1, 2019.

12. Thomas Edsall, "Is Wokeness 'Kryptonite for Democrats?'" *New York Times*, May 26, 2021.

13. *Oxford Dictionary*, "Mansplaining," April 3, 2020.

14. Katie Rogers, "Ivanka Trump Blames 'Cancel Culture' for Pulled Speech. College Says It Took a Stand," *New York Times*, June 7, 2020.

15. Caroline Vakil, "JD Vance Takes Aim at Culture Wars, Childless Politicians," *The Hill*, July 23, 2021.

16. Nick Gillespie, "Jonathan Rauch on Cancel Culture and the 'Unending Battle' for Free Speech," *Reason*, July 22, 2020.

17. Emily Ekins, "Poll: 62% of Americans Say They Have Political Views They're Afraid to Share," Cato Institute, July 22, 2020.

18. Nick Gillespie, "How To Tell If You're Being Canceled," *Reason*, December 4, 2020.

19. Emily Vogels and others, "Americans and 'Cancel Culture,'" Pew Research Center, May 19, 2021.

20. David Brooks, "We Just Saw How Minds Aren't Changed," *New York Times*, January 1, 2021.

21. Philip Sherwell, "The World According to Henry Kissinger," *The Telegraph*, May 21, 2011.

22. Minda Zetlin, "Workplace Harassment," *Inc.*, March/April, 2018.

23. Rachael Bade, "Dissension Inside the *Washington Post*," Politico *Playbook*, March 28, 2021.

24. Oliver Darcy, "*Washington Post*'s Top Editor Sends Memo to Staff after Backlash Over Handling of Reporter's Kobe Bryant Tweets," CNN, January 30, 2020.

25. Rachael Bade, "Dissension Inside the *Washington Post*," Politico *Playbook*, March 28, 2021.

26. Jeremy Barr, "*Washington Post* Reporter Felicia Sonmez Files Suit against the Newspaper and Top Editors Alleging Discrimination Over Past Coverage Ban," *Washington Post*, July 22, 2021.

27. Emily Peck, "Staffers Say Sexism Runs Deep at the *Washington Post*," *Huffington Post*, February 3, 2020.

28. Robin Bleiweis, "Quick Facts about the Gender Wage Gap," Center for American Progress," March 24, 2020.

29. Fiona Hill, *There Is Nothing for You Here: Finding Opportunity in the 21st Century* (Boston: Mariner Books, 2021).

30. Katelyn Fossett, "'If He Makes a Successful Return in 2024, Democracy's Done,'" Politico, October 8, 2021.

31. Charlotte Klein, "'I'm Afraid to Open Twitter': Next-Level Harassment of Female Journalists Is Putting News Outlets to the Test," *Vanity Fair*, March 26, 2021.

32. Tuugi Chuluun and Kevin Young, "Women at the Top of the World, Still Not at the Center," Brookings Institution, December 2020.

33. Ash Carter, "Taking—and Making—*Liberties*," Air Mail, August 15, 2020.

34. Some of this is drawn from Darrell M. West, *Divided Politics, Divided Nation: Hyperconflict in the Trump Era* (Brookings Institution Press, 2019).

35. *St. Louis Post-Dispatch*, "'Rape List' on Bathroom Walls Spurs Furor at Brown University," December 16, 1990, p. 9D; William Celis, "Date Rape and a List at Brown," *New York Times*, November 18, 1990.

36. Andre Perry, *Know Your Price: Valuing Black Lives and Property in America's Black Cities* (Brookings Institution Press, 2020).

37. Portions of this are drawn from Darrell M. West, "Who Is Getting a COVID-19 Vaccination?" Brookings *TechTank* (podcast), January 22, 2021.

38. West.

39. TV News Archive website, "Critical Race Theory," June 15, 2021.

40. Biba Adams, "Bill Banning Critical Race Theory in Public Schools Becomes Law," Yahoo News, May 4, 2021.

41. Charles Blow, "Demonizing Critical Race Theory," *New York Times*, June 13, 2021.

42. Ryan Lizza, Tara Palmeri, Eugene Daniels, and Rachael Bade, "'Critical' Poll Results," Politico *Playbook*, June 23, 2021.

43. Rashawn Ray and Alexandra Gibbons, "Why Are States Banning Critical Race Theory?" Brookings Institution *FixGov* (blog), July 2, 2021.

Chapter 10

1. Daniel Drezner, *The Ideas Industry: How Pessimists, Partisans, and Plutocrats Are Transforming the Marketplace of Ideas* (Oxford University Press, 2017).

2. Max Boot, "The Republican Plot to Steal the 2024 Election," *Washington Post*, June 1, 2021.

3. Barton Gellman, "Trump's Next Coup Has Already Begun," *The Atlantic*, December 6, 2021.

4. Luke Broadwater and Nick Corasaniti, "Jan. 6 Panel Targets Obscure Law Trump Tried to Use to Cling to Power," *New York Times*, December 5, 2021, p. 22.

5. Michael Wines, "As Washington Stews, State Legislatures Increasingly Shape American Politics," *New York Times*, August 29, 2021.

6. Mark Barabak, "He Warned Democracy Was in Peril. And That Was Before the Capitol Riots," *Los Angeles Times*, July 29, 2021.

7. Katelyn Fossett, "'If He Makes a Successful Return in 2024, Democracy's Done,'" Politico, October 8, 2021.

8. Darrell M. West, "It's Time to Abolish the Electoral College," Brookings Institution, October 15, 2019; and Norman Eisen and Norman Ornstein, "Seven Reasons to Think Senate Democrats Will Actually Change the Filibuster," *Washington Post*, September 13, 2021.

9. Richard Hasen, "Identifying and Minimizing the Risk of Election Subversion and Stolen Elections in the Contemporary United States," SSRN, September 18, 2021.

10. Gregory Koger, "The Origins of the 1887 Electoral College Act," *Mischiefs of Faction* (blog), January 4, 2021.

11. Quoted in Mike Allen, "Trump's Situation Room Shouting Match," *Axios AM*, June 28, 2021. Also see Bob Woodward and Robert Costa, *Peril* (New York: Simon & Schuster, 2021), p. xxi.

12. Michael Schmidt and Maggie Haberman, "Trump Aides Prepared Insurrection Act Order during Debate Over Protests," *New York Times*, June 25, 2021.

13. Darrell M. West, "Letters from Washington, D.C.," unpublished, 2021.

14. Jonathan Rauch, "How to Beat Trump & Co. in Their War on Truth," *New York Daily News*, May 22, 2021.

15. Tom Wheeler, Phil Verveer, and Gene Kimmelman, "New Digital Realities; New Oversight Solutions in the U.S.," Harvard Kennedy School Shorenstein Center, August, 2020.

16. Rashawn Ray and Andre Perry, "Why We Need Reparations for Black Americans," Brookings Institution, April 15, 2020.

17. Darrell M. West, "Digital Fingerprints Are Identifying Capitol Rioters," Brookings Institution, *TechTank* podcast, January 19, 2021.

18. Jose Pagliery and Roger Sollenberger, "Gaetz Paid Accused Sex Trafficker, Who Then Venmo'd Teen," Daily Beast, April 9, 2021.

19. Jose Pagliery and Roger Sollenberger, "Matt Gaetz's Wingman Paid Dozens of Young Women—and a 17-Year Old," Daily Beast, April 14, 2021.

20. Ryan Mac, Katie Notopoulos, Ryan Brooks, and Logan McDonald, "We Found Joe Biden's Secret Venmo," BuzzFeed News, May 14, 2021.

21. Darrell M. West, "How Employers Use Technology to Surveil Employees," Brookings Institution, *TechTank* (blog), January 5, 2021.

22. Kris Hirst, "What Did Cicero Mean by the Sword of Damocles?" ThoughtCo, April 12, 2018.

23. Darrell M. West, "How Employers Use Technology to Surveil Employees," Brookings Institution, *TechTank* (blog), January 5, 2021.

24. Harsh Munjal, "Machiavelli," Medium, April 7, 2020.

25. Hanson O'Haver, "How 'If You See Something, Say Something' Became Our National Motto," *Washington Post*, September 23, 2016.

Index

Figures and tables are indicated by "f" and "t" following page numbers.